GCSE Business and Communication Systems

The Revision Guide

It's another Quality Book from CGP

This book is a step-by-step guide to becoming an expert on GCSE Business and Communication Systems.

It contains all the really important stuff you need to know to answer the exam questions with confidence.

If you're after a book for Business and Communication Systems — this is it.

What CGP is all about

Our sole aim here at CGP is to produce the highest quality books — carefully written, immaculately presented and dangerously close to being funny.

Then we work our socks off to get them out to you — at the cheapest possible prices.

Contents

Section One — The Business Environment

Business Objectives 1
Measuring Business Success 2
Stakeholders 3
Organisational Structure 4
Team Working 6
Revision Summary for Section One 7

Section Two — Workplace Organisation & Data Management

Modern Working Practices 8
Office Layout 10
Call Centres 11
✓Health and Safety at Work 12
Data Capture — Manual Methods 13
Data Capture — Electronic Systems 14
Data Recording 15
Data Presentation 17
Accurate Data Storage 18
Security — Networks 19
Security — Hackers, Viruses and Copyright 20
Security — Data Protection 21
Efficiency of Systems 22
Revision Summary for Section Two 23

Section Three — Human Resources

Recruitment — Job Analysis 24
Recruitment — The Selection Process 25
Recruitment — Starting & Ending Contracts 26
Employment and the Law 27
Workplace Policies and Practices 28
Staff Training 29
Financial Rewards 30
Revision Summary for Section Three 32

Section Four — Communication

Purposes of Communication 33
Communication Channels 34
Communication — Networks and Hierarchies 35
Good and Bad Communication — The Effects 36
Written Communication 37
Electronic Communication 41
Corporate Image 42
Public Messaging Systems 43
Verbal Communication 44
Meetings 45
Choosing a Communication Channel 46
Communication Procedures and Policies 47
Revision Summary for Section Four 48

Section Five — ICT in the Business Environment

Computers and Networks 49
Networks — Different Configurations 51
Input Devices 52
Data Storage 54
Output Devices — Printers 56
Other Kinds of Output Device 58
ICT Systems 59
Revision Summary for Section Five 60

Section Six — Money Transfers & E-Commerce

Payment Systems 61
Telephone and Internet Banking 63
E-Commerce 64
Sales Documents 66
Revision Summary for Section Six 67

Section Seven — Computer Applications in the Business Environment

File Management 68
Word Processing Basics 69
Text Formatting and Editing 70
Improving Presentation 71
Editing Your Document 72
Word Processing — Advanced Features 73
Spreadsheets — Basics 75
Spreadsheets — Creating and Improving 76
Spreadsheets — Formulas 77
Spreadsheets — Graphs and Charts 78
Spreadsheet Models and Simulations 79
Databases — Creating and Editing One 80
Databases — Sorts and Queries 81
Databases — Reports 82
Graphics — Creating Images 83
Graphics — Image Manipulation 84
Desktop Publishing — Basics 85
DTP — Working with Frames 86
Presentation Software 87
Project Planning and Diary Management Software 89
Revision Summary for Section Seven 90

Index 91

Published by Coordination Group Publications Ltd.

Editors:
Keri Barrow, Katherine Reed,
Edward Robinson, Rachel Selway.

Contributors:
Colin Harber Stuart, David Morris,
Ali Palin, Jennifer Underwood,
Julie Wakeling, Keith Williamson.

*With thanks to Dawn Darby, Mike Shaw,
Victoria Skelton and Chrissy Williams for
the proofreading.*

ISBN-10: 1 84146 522 4
ISBN-13: 978 1 84146 522 7

Groovy website: www.cgpbooks.co.uk

Printed by Elanders Hindson Ltd, Newcastle upon Tyne.
Jolly bits of clipart from CorelDRAW®

Microsoft® and Windows® are either registered trademarks or trademarks of Microsoft Corporation in the United States and/or other countries.

Text, design, layout and original illustrations
© Coordination Group Publications Ltd. 2006
All rights reserved.

Glossary

Agenda — Document that sets out what will be discussed at a meeting.

BACS (Bankers Automated Clearing System) — A system where money is directly transferred from one bank account to another.

Cash flow — The money that flows in and out of a business.

Chain of command — The path decisions and communications have to go through in a business hierarchy.

Contract of employment — A legal agreement between the employer and the employee about the terms and conditions of a job.

Corporate image — The public reputation of a business.

Data encryption — Security software that scrambles data being sent over the internet into an unreadable code to protect it from hackers.

E-commerce — Business transactions that take place on the internet.

Electronic Data Interchange (EDI) — A system that links businesses directly to their bank account(s).

EFTPOS (Electronic Funds Transfer at Point of Sale) — Paying using a debit or credit card instead of cash.

EPOS (Electronic Point of Sale) — Laser scanners used to scan bar codes at shop checkouts.

Ergonomics — A way of designing office equipment and furniture so it's comfortable to use.

File extension — The last three letters of a file name used to identify the file type.

Fringe benefits — Extra benefits given to employees on top of their wages / salary.

Hierarchy — The levels in a business's organisational structure.

Horizontal communication — Communication along the same level of a business hierarchy.

Hot desking — When office workstations are not allocated to a particular person.

Intranet — A business's private computer network.

Job description — A written description of a job, including job title and main duties.

Job sharing — Two people sharing one job.

LAN (Local Area Network) — A small, local network of computers, e.g. in a school or office.

Market share — How much of the market a firm has compared to its competitors.

Memorandum (memo) — A formal document for internal communication.

Network — Two or more computers linked together.

Objective — An aim of the business.

Orphans — Small blocks of text that do not fit on the bottom of a page.

PAYE (pay as you earn) — Where an employer automatically deducts tax and national insurance from employees' pay.

Person specification — List of the skills, qualifications, experience and qualities of the ideal job candidate.

Profit — Total revenue minus total costs.

Private limited company (Ltd.) — A company owned by shareholders, but its shares can't be sold on the stock market.

Public limited company (PLC) — A company owned by shareholders and its shares can be sold on the stock market.

Salary — Wages for workers who are paid a fixed amount each month.

Span of control — The number of employees directly under one manager.

Stakeholder — Someone who is affected by a business (can be internal or external to the business).

Teleworking — Use of telecommunications so workers don't have to be in the office to do their work.

Time rate pay — Wages for workers who are paid an hourly rate.

Vertical communication — Communication up and down the levels of a business hierarchy, e.g. a message from a manager to an operative.

WAN (Wide Area Network) — A long range network which can connect together computers in different places.

Webstore — A website that sells goods or services.

WYSIWYG screen — "What you see is what you get." A screen display where the document looks exactly the same on screen as it does printed out.

SECTION ONE — THE BUSINESS ENVIRONMENT

Business Objectives

Here we go with Business and Communication Systems. This first section is more about business, than communication systems. These first few pages set the scene for the thrilling action that follows...

All Businesses Want to Make a Profit

An objective (or aim) is anything that the business wants to achieve.
Your objective in using this book is to get a better GCSE grade.

D'oh... forgot to make a profit

Typical Business Objectives

1) The most important objective is to make a profit in order to survive. If a business does not make a profit it will go bankrupt and have to close down.

Businesses will have other objectives which they might pursue too:

2) Some will try to be the biggest in their market.
3) Others will try to provide the highest quality product possible.
4) Some might aim to maximise sales.
5) Others might be more concerned with stability — maintaining their market share or a reasonable income.
6) Some will focus on expanding the business.
7) Other possible objectives include satisfying customers or trying to limit environmental damage.

Usually firms will only pursue these other objectives if it will help make a profit in the longer term. Firms might give up some profit for other objectives, but only if they have public-spirited owners.

Market share is how much of the market a firm has compared to its competitors.

Some businesses will not try to make a profit at all. This is either because they are a charity or they are in the public sector.

Charities and public sector businesses need to earn enough income to cover their costs. Any surplus is put back into the business.

The public sector includes everything that is owned by the government — things like the army or the police force.

Businesses Create Strategies to Achieve their Objectives

1) For a business to be successful it has to meet the objectives which it has set for itself. The way that the business co-ordinates the activities of its various departments in order to try and achieve these objectives is called a strategy.

2) The business will set itself success criteria — these are the targets it will use to measure whether or not it has met its objectives. These criteria are covered on the next page.

Stakeholders May Have Different Views about Success

Stakeholders are all the people who are affected by a business (see p. 3) including the owners, employees and local community. Different stakeholders may have different opinions about what the business needs to do in order to be successful. Some of these might be in conflict with the objectives the business sets itself, e.g. the local community might see job creation as a measure of the business's success, while the business's objective might be to cut costs.

I like to cover my costs with a blanket...

That's the first page done. It's really important you learn that list of objectives. Cover them up, then scribble down what you remember. Repeat until you've got them all. It's the only way.

Measuring Business Success

Businesses <u>measure</u> their <u>success</u> against their <u>business objectives</u>. <u>Profit</u> is the main way of measuring business success. But there are other ways it can be measured.

Owners and Shareholders Want Profit

<u>Profit</u> is a <u>key measure</u> of <u>success</u> for private sector businesses.

1) <u>Owners</u> and <u>shareholders</u> often want to <u>maximise profit</u> because they benefit directly from an increase in their personal wealth, or by receiving a dividend, i.e. a share of the profits.

2) Maximising profit can be good for employees if they get a <u>pay rise</u> or a <u>bonus</u> because of it.

Profit = total revenue – total costs

Success can be Measured by Job Creation

1) <u>Job creation</u> means providing more <u>employment</u> for people. It is important to the government because jobs create wealth in the economy and help to raise the <u>standard of living</u>. This creates demand for more goods and services.

2) <u>Job security</u> is another measure of success. Job security is important to workers because they need to be able to <u>plan for their future</u> — for example, if they want to buy a house. Employers also want to provide job security because it <u>motivates staff</u> and makes them more <u>productive</u>.

3) Job creation and security are linked to <u>profitability</u>. The more profitable the business, the more likely the business is to pay well, provide opportunities for promotion, improve conditions of service and expand its workforce.

Market Share is also a Measure of Success

A business's market share = $\dfrac{\text{the business's sales}}{\text{total sales in that market}} \times 100$

1) Market share is important to a business because it shows its <u>market power</u> and how successful it is compared to its <u>competitors</u>.

2) Increasing market share often means <u>greater profitability</u> and <u>job security</u> for workers.

Businesses want Positive Cash Flow

1) Cash flow is the <u>flow</u> of all <u>money into</u> and <u>out</u> of the <u>business</u>. When a firm sells its products, money flows in. When it buys materials or pays its workers, money flows out.

2) Having a <u>positive</u> cash flow (more money coming in than going out) is <u>critical</u> because a negative cash flow results in suppliers or workers being unpaid.

3) <u>Negative</u> cash flow cannot continue in the long term. Eventually the business will <u>fail</u> and go <u>bankrupt</u>, resulting in <u>losses</u> for the owners and <u>unemployment</u> for the staff.

Shopping — guaranteed to give me negative cash flow...

The basic idea here is that <u>success</u> can be <u>measured</u> — but there are different ways of measuring it. Remember that <u>profit</u> is usually the most <u>important</u> measure of success and that positive cash flow is really important too. Without money coming in a business will go up the spout.

Stakeholders

Everyone who is affected by a business is called a stakeholder because they have a stake in what the business does. There are two types of stakeholder: internal stakeholders and external stakeholders.

Internal Stakeholders are Inside the Firm

1) The owners are the most important stakeholders. They get to decide what happens to a business and make a profit if the business is successful. Limited companies are owned by their shareholders — each of them owns a small part of the company.

2) Employees are also internal stakeholders. They are interested in their job security and promotion prospects — they also want to earn a decent wage and have pleasant working conditions.

External Stakeholders are Outside the Firm

1) Customers want high quality products at low prices. They also want good customer service.

2) Suppliers are who the business buys raw materials and other products from. Good communication with suppliers is important to ensure that the right product is delivered at the right time for the right price. Many businesses use supply chain management systems, or e-commerce to improve efficiency.

3) The local community want good jobs, and improved local facilities, but not at the expense of environmental pollution. Good Public Relations (PR) improves the image of a business. Poor PR can be very damaging, and sometimes results in consumers boycotting products.

4) The government receives taxes when the business makes a profit. Failure to pay the right taxes can result in substantial fines and even the closure of a business.

Conflict between Stakeholders can Constrain a Firm

1) An owner's desire to maximise profits can cause conflict with staff if they increase the profits by reducing pay, changing working practices or cutting jobs.

2) Conflict between managers and workers can lead to industrial action. Some workers are members of trade unions, which negotiate with employers over pay and conditions, and may organise strikes. Industrial action is bad for the business because it can stop production, let down customers and lose the company money.

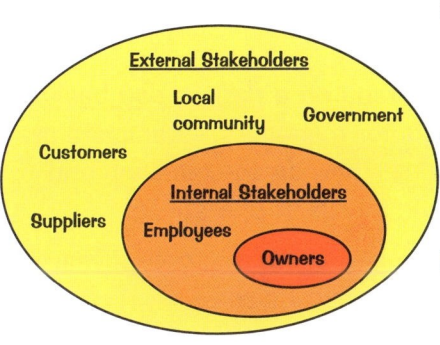

3) Poor communication between internal stakeholders can lead to reduced morale and a loss in productivity or competitiveness.

4) Businesses want to provide customer satisfaction, but not at any price. This puts a constraint on products which must satisfy the customer but still be profitable.

5) Governments introduce laws to protect customers and workers and make sure that competition is fair. This can put a constraint on businesses — for example, it is illegal to advertise cigarettes in magazines.

Stakeholders — the essential bbq tool...

It is not just the owners who have an interest in a business, the nosy neighbours do too. Make a list of all the stakeholders and give an example of how each one can constrain what a business does.

SECTION ONE — THE BUSINESS ENVIRONMENT

Organisational Structure

A hierarchy — the posh term for a pecking order. That basically means the boss at the top and the workers at the bottom.

The Larger the Business the Bigger the Hierarchy

1) Sole traders usually have no employees — there is no hierarchy. A large public limited company (PLC) may have several layers in its hierarchy.

2) At the top of the hierarchy are the owners — shareholders in a limited company. The shareholders appoint the directors, who are in overall day-to-day control of the company.

3) The directors appoint the managers. Managers appoint and organise operatives who do the everyday work of the business.

Hierarchy can Affect Communication

The hierarchy of a firm affects the chain of command — the path decisions and communications have to go through.

1) A hierarchical firm has lots of layers. Communication can be difficult and slow because there are lots of layers to go through. But employees know who to go to for decisions on different issues.

2) A flat hierarchy has fewer layers. It can make communication clearer and more efficient. But it means that managers can get overwhelmed by having too many people reporting to them.

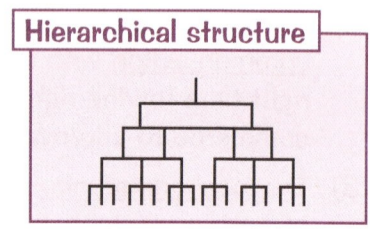

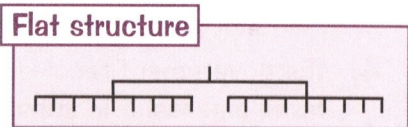

Directors Decide the Strategy of the Company

1) In most PLCs the shareholders also own shares in many other companies. So shareholders delegate responsibility for the general direction — the strategy — of the business to the directors. The directors decide on strategy and targets at regular board meetings. The directors can be removed from their job by the shareholders.

2) The top director is called the Chair of the Board. He/she runs the board meetings. The next most important director is the Managing Director. He/she runs the business between the main board meetings.

3) The directors delegate responsibility for implementing their strategy on a day-to-day basis to the managers. A large business will have senior, middle and junior managers. Managers are responsible for the operatives carrying out their tasks properly. They do the planning and organising. Each manager will have responsibility for a specific group of operatives.

4) In some businesses there will be a level of supervisors between managers and operatives. Supervisors usually look after specific projects or small teams of operatives.

5) Operatives are given specific tasks to perform by managers or supervisors.

Chain of command — classic QVC jewellery...

Hierarchy is all to do with how many levels there are in a company and the amount of power individuals have at each level. Make sure you learn the different levels of workers in a hierarchy.

SECTION ONE — THE BUSINESS ENVIRONMENT

Organisational Structure

Firms organise themselves in different ways to get the most out of their physical, human and financial resources — this page tells you about the three main types of organisational structure.

You can Organise by Function...

You get this a lot with limited companies. Each department does one part of the work of the business. The main advantage of functional organisation is that specialists can concentrate on their particular job. The main disadvantage is that different departments may not work well together. For it to work there needs to be good communication between the departments.

Finance Department
The finance department prepares detailed and accurate financial information which is used by other departments. They use specialist financial software applications for recording receipts and payments, and for payroll. Financial managers work with sales people to check progress against forecasts and with production staff to monitor and control costs.

Human Resources (HR) Department
Human Resources Management (HRM) is responsible for getting the right number of employees with the right skills at the right time. HRM recruits, trains or dismisses workers by liaising with other departments. They need to know which departments will need staff, how many and when.

Production Department
The production department is responsible for manufacturing the product, ordering and storing raw materials. Communication with sales staff is key to ensuring production capacity is matched to demand.

Marketing Department
The marketing department figures out what customers want and how best to sell it to them. The marketing department works with production staff to ensure the products meet customers' needs.

...Or you can Organise by Product...

1) A product-based structure splits the organisation into different sectors for the different products. Each sector is likely to be organised by function.
2) This is common with large manufacturers who make lots of different products.
3) The main advantage is that managers can make decisions that are relevant to each product division. A big disadvantage is that there can be a wasteful duplication of resources between divisions — each product division will have their own departments for functions like finance, marketing and production.

...Or Organise by Region

This is usual for multinational businesses. The divisions may be regional or national. The main advantage of it is that spreading management between regions makes day-to-day control easier. A disadvantage is that there can be a wasteful duplication of resources between regions — each region is likely to have its own departments for functions like finance, marketing and production.

Duplication is wasteful, duplication is wasteful...
E-businesses, where all business is done electronically, often don't use any of these traditional organisational structures because it doesn't suit the way they do business.

Team Working

Each department works as a team to complete tasks and achieve objectives. Big teams can be broken down into smaller teams to do day-to day tasks.

Departments must Work with Each Other

1) Managers, supervisors and operatives work together as a team to achieve their department's objectives which help to achieve the company's objectives.
2) Different departments need to work together to meet the needs of the customer. E.g. the sales department will process a customer's order, the production department will manufacture and deliver the order, and the finance department will invoice the customer.
3) In order to work together effectively, the role and responsibilities of each department need to be clear. There also needs to be good communication between and within teams.

Project Teams may be Formed for Specific Tasks

1) Businesses often form special project teams for a specific task or project.
2) The team is made up of employees from different departments and the team is led by a Project Manager who has overall responsibility for the project.

Teams follow a Series of Steps

1) **CONFIRM WHAT NEEDS TO BE DONE** — Agreeing what needs to be achieved.
2) **AGREE RESPONSIBILITIES** — Deciding who is responsible for what.
3) **WORK WITH OTHERS** — Working with others to achieve shared objectives.
4) **CARRY OUT TASKS** — Completing each part of the task.
5) **SUGGEST WAYS OF IMPROVING** — Monitoring progress and making improvements.

Business Systems Help Teamworking

1) Individuals need to be able to communicate and share information to work effectively together in a team.
2) Business systems and technology help enable good communication and team working — even when people do not work in the same office. For example, databases, websites and intranets help workers gather and share information.

For more on the internet and intranets see p.50.

Businesses put Effort into Team Building

Businesses often put considerable effort into building team spirit and communication. E.g.

1) Using ice breakers to help people to get to know one another.
2) Conferences — e.g. where managers from different parts of a business meet to discuss and exchange views on issues that affect them.
3) Management team building activities, often involving outdoor pursuits.

The A-team — for when no-one else can help...

Team members need to co-operate and communicate to work efficiently. Make sure you know the five steps teams have to follow — without these, teams wouldn't be able to complete their tasks.

SECTION ONE — THE BUSINESS ENVIRONMENT

Revision Summary for Section One

Okay, so that's the first section over with — now it's time to see how much you can remember. Have a bash at these questions. If you can do them all, pat yourself on the back and feel smug. If you can't, then go back and look at the section again and keep plugging away until you can answer them all. Yes, I know it's a pain but life's like that — and after all, it's the only way you're going to get ready for the exam.

1) What is the most important objective for a business?
2) Give three other objectives apart from profit that businesses might pursue.
3) Do charities aim to make a profit?
4) What are stakeholders?
5) Name two ways business success can be measured.
6) How do you calculate profit?
7) Why is job security important for workers?
8) What is market share?
9) Do firms want positive or negative cash flow?
10) Name six types of stakeholder and say whether they are internal or external.
11) Which is the most important stakeholder and why?
12) Why is good Public Relations (PR) important?
13) How can the government constrain what a business does?
14) Who is at the bottom of the business hierarchy?
    a) shareholders   b) operatives   c) plankton
15) Why is communication in a hierarchical firm sometimes slow?
16) How many layers does a flat hierarchy have?
    a) many   b) few   c) 71
17) What is the role of supervisors?
18) What are the three main ways that businesses can be structured?
19) Say which type of organisational structure would be most suitable for these companies:
    a) a transnational oil company with offices all over the world,
    b) a limited company that manufactures washing machine parts.
20) What is the role of the HR department?
21) What is the role of the marketing department?
22) What are project teams?
23) What are the five steps teams follow?
24) List two ways businesses try to encourage team building.

SECTION ONE — THE BUSINESS ENVIRONMENT

Modern Working Practices

Until recently a typical job involved working full time on a permanent contract. But flexible working is becoming more popular — many staff no longer have to work the traditional office hours 9 to 5.

Many People now Work Part-Time or Flexitime

1) Some workers only work part-time, which means they do fewer hours than full time workers. This might be just a couple of hours a week or 30 hours a week.

2) In some workplaces two people share one job — one person may work from Monday to Wednesday lunch time and the other will work the rest of the week. This is called job sharing.

3) Some workplaces have a flexitime system which allows workers to vary their work hours. Workers have to work a set number of hours in a day or week and have to be in work during a core time such as between 10 am and 3 pm, but they can choose when they start and finish.

Flexible Working means Businesses Keep Skilled Workers

Advantages for employees

1) The main advantage of part-time or flexible working for employees is that it makes it easier for people to balance working with other commitments, e.g. looking after children or caring for other people.

2) Students can get a part time job to help finance their studies.

Advantages for employers

1) Part-time and flexible working also has advantages for employers. It allows businesses to keep skilled staff when the employee's circumstances change without having to recruit or train new staff.

2) It makes it easier for employers, such as retailers, to have more staff available at busy times. So, for example, if a business has its busiest period at lunchtime, it can arrange for most of the part-time staff to work between 11 am and 3 pm.

But Part-Time Work can be Complicated

1) Employees may find it difficult to agree working hours that suit themselves and their employers.

2) They may have to work full time if they get promoted.

3) Their salary will be reduced in proportion to the number of hours or days that they work.

4) Unless there are good communications between job sharers, time is wasted finding out what the other person in the arrangement has done.

Flexible working — get a job as a yoga instructor...

One job, two people — job sharing is pretty simple. Make sure you know the advantages and disadvantages of flexible working for both employees and employers.

Modern Working Practices

It's not just working hours that are becoming more flexible. Businesses are becoming more flexible about how staff carry out their jobs and where they actually do their work.

New Ways of Working are Being Introduced

Generally employees are becoming more productive at work, because of better equipment, new technology and new processes. For example, it's now much quicker to write letters because of word processing and templates, which means more letters can be created in a day. Employees have time to carry out more tasks and use different skills — this is called being multi-skilled.

1) An advantage of having multi-skilled workers for businesses is that they need fewer staff to carry out the same amount of work. It allows other staff to cover for others when they are absent from work.

2) One advantage for employees of being multi-skilled is it can help make their job more interesting. Working for a business that likes its staff to be multi-skilled means there are more opportunities for training and learning new skills. There can be better chances of promotion as employees have more skills.

3) However, training is expensive for businesses and takes time. When an employee leaves, it can be difficult to find a replacement who has the same range of skills.

> When new ways of working are introduced employers will re-train current employees to use new equipment, ICT systems or to do new tasks. This is called re-skilling.

ICT is Changing How Staff do their Work

1) Hot desking is when workstations in an office are not allocated to a particular person. Instead workers are given work space to use to suit the task they are working on. If all the computers are on the same network with the same software it reduces the need for people to have their own desk. Hot desking helps businesses to reduce their costs because they don't need to give permanent desk space and equipment to staff who don't always need it.

2) Improvements in telecommunications has led to teleworking (working from home). Employees can work from home or when travelling by using the internet, email, mobile phones and laptops.

3) Tele-conferencing is when people use computer or telephone facilities to hold meetings without having to travel to the same place. Instead they hold the meeting over the phone or by using a video link. This saves time and travelling costs, especially if the business has overseas offices.

Specialists and Consultants Can be Used for Expertise

1) Some businesses use external specialists and consultants to make them more flexible. They keep a core of permanent staff to carry out the main tasks and use specialists or consultants when they need expertise their core staff don't have.

2) For example, when hiring new staff many businesses use recruitment agencies. It takes away the hassle for the business of having to advertise the job and deal with the applications. The business only pays for the specialist skills and knowledge when it actually needs them.

Hot desking — great for warming up your lunch...

Three main points here for you to learn — technology has affected how employees do their job, where employees do their job and what tasks they actually do.

Office Layout

The layout of an office can affect how well staff do their jobs. If the layout doesn't suit the type of work the business does it can lead to problems.

There are Two Main Types of Office Layout

Open Plan Offices

1) The office is one big space that is partitioned into smaller offices, usually using screens. Often different level staff all work together, so managers aren't separated from their staff.

2) An advantage of open plan offices is it's easier to supervise staff. They can also improve communication between staff as they are sat together and can see each other.

3) The main disadvantage is that open plan offices can be noisy which affects concentration. Another disadvantage is that staff sometimes feel they are being watched all the time and are not trusted to do their work properly. This can lead to low morale.

Cellular Offices

1) This is the traditional style of office layout. The office is divided up into smaller rooms, with doors that can be closed. These smaller rooms hold a few workers or just one person.

2) Cellular offices are an advantage when staff need quiet or privacy to do their work. They are also good for security as they can be locked to protect valuable or confidential things.

3) A disadvantage of cellular office layout is that it can make supervision of junior staff more difficult. It can also result in less communication between employees.

What the Business Does Influences Office Layout

1) For example, if the work of the business requires a high level of security, such as a bank branch, then this will be an important factor in the design. A bank needs to provide a secure environment for employees without the physical barriers putting off customers.

2) Another example is call centres. These are usually designed to fit as many operators into the office space as possible, so there's the maximum number of people to take calls (see p.11).

3) The nature of the tasks individual staff carry out sometimes affects the layout of the office. E.g. managers often have private offices because they need privacy for confidential meetings, but call centre staff can be in the same space together as they are doing the same work.

Ergonomics also Influence Office Layout

1) If employees are uncomfortable in their workplace they will not work as efficiently as they could.

2) Furniture like chairs and desks can be ergonomically designed — this means the furniture is designed to fit the shape of the body so it is comfortable for the user.

3) Workstations need to be designed and set up so they don't contribute to back pain, eye strain or repetitive strain injury for the staff using them.

4) The design of office furniture and physical working conditions are also influenced by Health and Safety requirements (see p.12).

Cellular office — a lock on the door and bars on the window...

Office layout is a bit dull, but at least it's straightforward. Cover the page and write down the two types of office layout, then list their advantages and disadvantages.

Call Centres

In recent years businesses have reorganised themselves to become more cost effective and efficient in dealing with more customers at less cost. Call centres are one way of doing this.

Call Centres are Becoming Increasingly Common

1) A call centre is a centralised office which makes and receives phone calls from customers. Large businesses often have their own call centres. Smaller businesses often pay professional call centres to handle their calls for them.

2) Often call centres are open longer than normal business hours. This means businesses have access to customers outside the main working day — even at weekends. This improves customer service and increases the possibility of making sales.

3) Call centres have been used to replace local branches or offices. Having fewer local branches or offices can save a business a lot of money. Banks and insurance companies use call centres for many functions. For example, customers can use call centres to check their bank balance, make payments or arrange loans when their bank branch is closed.

4) Call centres can also support the sales and marketing functions of a business. They can make phone calls to customers or potential customers to ask if they are interested in buying their products — double glazing is a good example of this.

They can be Convenient for Customers and Businesses

1) The main advantage of call centres for customers is that it is easier to get hold of the business when they need to. Customers, especially in rural areas, do not need to make special trips to town to buy goods or visit the bank for routine transactions.

2) Customers can contact the business when it suits them, e.g. in the evenings or at weekends.

3) The main advantages of call centres for businesses is that they are more cost efficient — it is cheaper to have one or two large call centres than many smaller branches. Businesses can save on labour costs and need to buy or rent fewer buildings.

4) Call centres can be set up anywhere as long as the call centre operatives have access to all the customer information they need. Many businesses now have their call centres overseas in countries like India where it is much cheaper to hire staff.

Can you tell me my bank balance please.

Some People Don't Like Call Centres

1) Some customers prefer to deal with staff on a face-to-face basis. They feel that call centres are impersonal and get very frustrated when they are put on hold or kept in a phone queue.

2) Many people object to call centres being based overseas. They do not like jobs being taken away from the UK.

3) Being a call centre operative can be a rubbish job — you have to spend all day on the phone, you have targets you have to meet and some customers can be very rude. The operators often get fed up with this and leave. This increases recruitment and training costs for businesses.

Don't leave me hanging on the telephone...

Call centres get some people very wound up, especially when they phone you in the middle of dinner. But most businesses think they're good — for them it means lower costs.

SECTION TWO — WORKPLACE ORGANISATION & DATA MANAGEMENT

Health and Safety at Work

There are laws to help ensure that people don't get ill or injured at work. The laws make health and safety the responsibility of both the employer and employees.

Employers Need to Follow Health and Safety Legislation

1) The Health and Safety at Work Act 1974 is the main law. It requires all employers and employees to take responsibility for health and safety. Businesses have to provide a safe working environment, make sure that all equipment is safe and maintained and provide protective clothing if it is needed. The Health and Safety Executive (HSE) enforces health and safety laws.

2) The Display Screen Equipment Regulations 1992 set rules about the safe use of computers.

> **Display Screen Equipment Regulations 1992**
>
> Employers have to:
> 1) Analyse workstations, and assess and reduce risks. Employers need to check that computer equipment is safe. If it isn't they need to take action to make it safe.
> 2) Ensure workstations meet minimum requirements. This includes providing necessary equipment, e.g. an anti-glare screen.
> 3) Provide free eye-tests to all staff who regularly use VDUs as part of their job.
> 4) Provide health and safety training and information — so that employees can take action themselves to reduce the health risks.

Go ahead, make my day. I'll report you under the 1992 Workplace Regulations.

3) Many businesses have an accident book that is used to report accidents that happen in the workplace. This means accidents can be investigated and hazards identified to prevent future accidents. It is the employee's responsibility to report an accident.

Computer Use can Cause Three Main Problems

1) Repetitive strain injury (RSI) is a general term for aches, pains and muscle or tendon damage resulting from overuse of a keyboard or mouse. Some people call it upper limb disorder (ULD).

2) Spending too long in front of a VDU can cause eye strain and headaches. The glare from the screen can make it hard for the eyes to focus properly.

3) Circulation, fitness and back problems might result from sitting all day in front of a computer rather than walking around. This is more of a long-term health problem.

Employers and Employees are Responsible for the Solutions

1) Employers should allow employees to take regular breaks from computer work. Looking away from the screen, walking around and exercising your fingers and hands can also help to reduce the health risks. Employees need to make sure their posture is correct.

2) Employers have a responsibility to provide the correct equipment, e.g. a screen filter to reduce VDU glare for computer users or ear protection for workers who have to use noisy machinery.

3) Employers and employees both need to make sure equipment is arranged properly to reduce the risk of injury or illness. This includes desks, chairs, keyboards and VDUs.

The accident book — might be a good read...

Employers and employees have to work together to create a safe working environment. Draw a table with the problems computers can cause in one column and the solutions in another column.

SECTION TWO — WORKPLACE ORGANISATION & DATA MANAGEMENT

Data Capture — Manual Methods

Data capture is the way that information is gathered and put on a computer system. What fun.

Data Capture turns Information into Data

Data capture is sometimes called data collection. It's a two-part process:
1) The information has to be obtained, recorded and then converted into a form suitable for use with the computer system.
2) The data has to be entered (input) onto the computer using an input device.

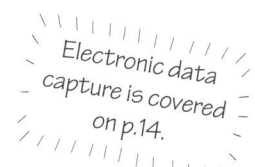
Electronic data capture is covered on p.14.

Manual Data Capture Needs People to do it

Manual data capture needs a person to record the data on to a paper form or electronic form. There are three main methods of data capture — data capture forms, questionnaires and interviews.

Data capture forms

1) Data capture forms are the most common way of obtaining and recording data. Manual data capture forms are usually paper-based forms where someone records information in a preset way, e.g. the application form for a course or to join a mailing list.

2) Some data capture forms are designed for using with an OMR device (Optical Mark Recognition). This type of form usually has a choice of boxes to fill in. The OMR device scans the completed form, detects which boxes have been filled in and inputs the information into a computer. This type of data capture form is used for multiple-choice answer sheets and computerised school registers.

3) Many e-commerce sites ask customers to provide their details when buying goods. The fields that are filled in are a type of data capture.

To make sure you get the information you need it's really important that the data capture form is carefully designed. Badly designed forms can cause lots of problems. Here's how to design one:
- Keep the layout simple. Leave enough space to write answers, and don't put answer boxes too close together — or information can get put in the wrong box by mistake.
- Instructions on how to complete the form should be written in simple language. It should be obvious to the user what to do.
- Keep the amount of information requested to a minimum. There's no point asking for information which won't be used.
- The form should be checked for accuracy and completeness before it is printed. Then it should be pre-tested with a small sample of people to check that it's easy to use.

Questionnaires

Questionnaires work in a similar way to data capture forms — people are asked a set list of questions and the answers are recorded on a form. Questionnaires can ask quantitive questions, e.g. 'How many rabbits do you buy each month?'. Or qualitative questions, e.g. 'What do you think of CGP's rabbits?'

Interviews

In interviews a set of questions will be asked verbally to an interviewee, and the interviewee's responses are recorded by the interviewer.

Manual Methods have Advantages

Sometimes using a manual method to obtain data is necessary because the information can only be obtained using a manual data capture form — such as personal details. It's also usually cheaper than electronic methods as less hardware and software are needed.

Data was captured in episode #153...

Captain Picard and Commander Riker had to rescue him from a tar monster, with the help of the Klingons. Not really, it just sounded better than "Learn the three ways data can be captured."

SECTION TWO — WORKPLACE ORGANISATION & DATA MANAGEMENT

Data Capture — Electronic Systems

Some organisations gather the data they need using <u>electronic methods</u>. These allow them to control stock, record sales, collect money owing to them and make payments electronically.

Electronic Systems Make Stock Control Easier...

1) The best example of how electronic systems are used in business is when you buy goods from <u>shops</u>. Most products have a <u>bar code</u> on them or their packaging — like tins of beans, clothes labels and this book.

I said bar codes, not baa codes. Ahahaha-haha. Ahahaha-haha.

2) A <u>bar code</u> is a pattern of thick and thin black lines. It <u>contains information</u> about the product, and ends with a <u>check digit</u>, so the computer can validate that the data is correct. Bar codes are read at the Electronic Point of Sale.

3) <u>Electronic Point of Sale</u> (often called <u>EPOS</u>) is the high-tech tills and <u>laser scanners</u> in shops. When goods are passed over the laser scanner, the data contained on the bar code is passed, electronically, to the store's computer system. The store's computer system contains the <u>product file</u>, <u>price file</u> and <u>stock file</u> for each item with a bar code. The computer system will send the price to the till, which processes and prints the customer's bill and receipt.

4) The computer then <u>reduces</u> the <u>recorded stock level</u> of the product. When stock falls to a pre-set amount (the reorder level), an order for more stock is automatically sent.

...And mean Payments can be Made Without Cash

1) <u>Electronic fund transfer at point of sale</u> — <u>EFTPOS</u> for short — is when customers are allowed to pay using their <u>debit or credit card</u> instead of cash.

2) Debit and credit cards have a <u>magnetic stripe</u> on the back. The operator <u>swipes</u> the card through a <u>magnetic reader</u>, which tells the computer the banking details of the card's owner, such as the account number and branch code. A payment request is then sent to the bank via the telephone network. If the card is valid, the payment is <u>authorised</u> and the funds are transferred from the customer's account to the shop's account.

3) A <u>potential problem</u> of this system is <u>card fraud</u> — when the goods are paid for using someone else's card. <u>Chip and PIN</u> is used to help reduce the risk of card fraud — card details are held on a <u>microchip</u> on the card, and the card holder has to enter their <u>personal identification number</u> (PIN) to authorise payment using their debit or credit card.

4) <u>Bankers Automated Clearing System</u> (<u>BACS</u>) is a way of electronically transferring money directly from one bank account to another through the telephone network. Many companies use this system to pay employees and suppliers. (See p.62 for more on BACS.)

Electronic Systems have Advantages for Businesses

1) Internet businesses use BACS to allow <u>customers to pay</u> for goods they have ordered. It's good for internet retailers because they are paid before they have to deliver the goods. It can also lead to <u>lower costs</u> as they need fewer staff to process bank transfers and avoid bad debts.

2) Using electronic systems can help businesses <u>reduce</u> the <u>time and cost</u> of activities such as sending invoices and paying bills. Also, paying staff directly with BACS is <u>safer</u> than paying them in cash and is cheaper because they do not have to pay security firms to deliver the cash.

3) Electronic systems make it much <u>easier</u> for warehouses to <u>monitor and control</u> their <u>stock levels</u> and process customer orders.

I say EPOS you say EFTPOS...

Electronic systems are great for businesses as they can <u>speed up</u> processes and payments. But they can be <u>expensive</u> to invest in. Make sure you know what EPOS, EFTPOS and BACS stand for.

Data Recording

Businesses need to record the data they collect so it can be analysed, shared or used in future. Manual or electronic methods can be used to record data — the next two pages tell you how.

Manual Methods are Still Used for Market Research

1) Businesses carry out primary market research to find out information from customers, such as what customers think of their products or services and how often they use them. It's important businesses get accurate information from their market research — so how the answers are recorded can make a big difference.

2) The data can be collected manually by questionnaires, surveys or interviews — e.g. the people in high streets with clipboards are usually doing market research. It can also be collected by observation, or by using electronic products e.g. data logging.

3) The questions are designed to get the specific information the business needs. Many of the questions are closed. This means that there are a limited number of answers a person can give. The results can be easily recorded on a data capture form (see p.13) or by using tally charts, which are another type of data capture.

Tally charts

A tally chart is a grid that helps to clearly show information as it is collected. Lines are used to show numbers as a running tally.

Question	0-5 times	Total 0-5 times	6-15 times	Total 6-15 times	More than 15 times	Total 15+ times
1) How often do you bang your head against the wall when listening to James Blunt?	|||	3	##### ///	8	##### ##### ////	14

Word Processing is One Way of Recording Data

1) Word processing software, such as Microsoft® Word, can be used by businesses to record data in the form of letters, memorandums, reports, tables, agendas and notices.

2) It can be used to produce a standardised version of a document, using a template. A business can set up a template so that all its business letters or memos look the same.

3) If letters such as payment reminders have to be sent out in large numbers most of the wording will be the same in all the letters. The template will include all the standard wording and there will be space to include the amount owing and the specific customer's details. You can use mail merge to put in the details for each customer (see p.74 for more on mail merge).

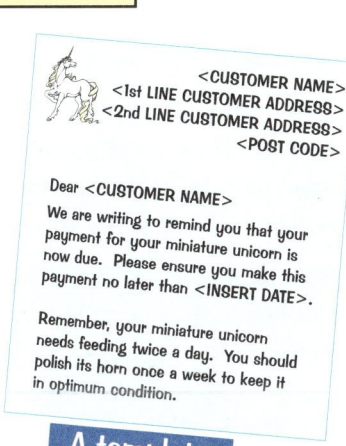

A template

Recording data — just set the video...

Word processing is great for recording data that doesn't need lots of calculations or fancy pictures. There's more exciting stuff on word processing later — this is a taste of the excitement to come.

SECTION TWO — WORKPLACE ORGANISATION & DATA MANAGEMENT

Data Recording

Word processing isn't the only way to record data — here are <u>three more</u> computer applications you can use to record data.

Spreadsheets are Used for Numbers and Graphs

1) <u>Financial</u> and <u>numerical information</u>, such as sales figures, are normally recorded on spreadsheet applications like Microsoft® Excel or Lotus 1-2-3.

2) Organising the information in tables of columns and rows makes it <u>easier to read and understand</u>. Spreadsheets can be used to do <u>calculations</u> and to turn the data into <u>graphs</u> and <u>charts</u>.

3) Although spreadsheets can also be used for simple lists, such as names and addresses or products, they are not very good for doing complex searches and sorting data in different ways.

Sales figures for miniature unicorn items		
	A	B
1	Item	June Sales
2	Horn Polish	19,568
3	Mini hoof pick	2,006
4	Dragon-proof reins	79
5	Mane shampoo	1,973

Databases Make it Easy to Sort and Search Data

1) Many organisations record data in databases. A database is basically an electronic collection of information or records. Databases can hold <u>huge amounts</u> of data and are easy to <u>sort</u> and <u>search</u> for certain information.

2) Information in databases can be <u>sorted</u> into <u>alphabetical</u> or <u>numerical</u> order. Reports can be printed or viewed on screen in a way which makes it easy to understand the information.

3) Businesses can use databases to <u>store data</u> about their customers and their suppliers. The databases can be used to <u>produce lists</u> of different groups who have particular characteristics, such as everyone who bought a certain product within the last six months or customers who have good or bad payment records.

Table 1: Customer Orders		
Name	Date ordered	Addres
F Dettori	30/01/97	Glebe F
W Carson	06/09/89	7 Some
A P McCoy	31/04/04	Chestnu
D Francis	17/08/84	Murdoc

Record 3 of 12973

DTP Produces Professional Looking Documents

1) Although word processing is very good for standard documents it is not good enough for complicated documents such as catalogues, brochures, newspapers and advertising features. Special <u>desk top publishing</u> (<u>DTP</u>) software is used instead.

2) By using DTP software such as QuarkXPress®, Adobe® InDesign® or Microsoft® Publisher it is possible to produce newsletters, leaflets, notices or worksheets that contain <u>complex graphics</u>, e.g. flowcharts. It has <u>better facilities</u> to design pages, add colour, scan in diagrams and alter images. DTP also has the facilities to produce organisation charts.

What's this page about — search me...

It's important for businesses to pick the <u>most appropriate way</u> to record their data — recording a letter in a spreadsheet just isn't cricket. Shut the book and scribble down the <u>four</u> different types of software programs that can be used to record data and the type of data that they suit.

SECTION TWO — WORKPLACE ORGANISATION & DATA MANAGEMENT

Data Presentation

Data can be presented in different ways — e.g. a talk, a written presentation, a massive spreadsheet. The four main ways to present data are covered in this page...

The Audience Affects How Data is Presented

1) It's important to think about the needs of the audience when deciding how to present data. For example, if you're presenting the data to people who already know a lot about the subject, then you could send them a written report. But if you're presenting the data to people with little knowledge of the subject, a face to face talk might be better so you can answer any questions and explain difficult terms.

2) The type of data also influences the way it is presented. For example, if you're presenting some basic information, a written memo or notice might be appropriate. But if you have to communicate some complicated data, it might be better to present the information in a detailed report.

There are Four Main Ways to Present Data

1 **WRITTEN** — data can be presented as a written document, e.g. reports, letters, handouts, memos, notices.

2 **NUMERICAL** — data presented in tables and calculations. Numerical presentation suits data like sales figures and financial data. Numerical data is often supported by a written account or graphs of what the figures show to help people understand it.

3 **ORAL** — data is presented as a talk. Presenting data in this way is good when you want to check that people have understood it, because it gives the audience a chance to ask questions. Oral presentations are often supported by slides, handouts or demonstrations.

4 **VISUAL** — there are different ways data can be presented visually — it could be as a graph or chart, pictures, photos, a demonstration, slides or handouts. Showing data visually often helps people to understand an idea better and can be used as part of a written or numerical presentation or to support a talk.

Often when you present data, you use more than one method — for example, a person giving a talk may also provide written handouts.

Accurate Preparation is Really Important

1) When preparing a presentation it is important to make sure that there are no spelling mistakes, the punctuation and grammar are correct and the ideas in the presentation are clear.

2) If the presentation is full of spelling mistakes or the ideas are unclear it will lose its effectiveness. The audience may not understand it, and it may give a poor impression of the presenter or the business.

Ambassador, with all this talk of data, you are spoiling us...

It's important to remember that how data is presented affects its impact on the audience. Badly presented information has less of an impact — the audience are more likely to get bored.

SECTION TWO — WORKPLACE ORGANISATION & DATA MANAGEMENT

Accurate Data Storage

Accuracy is really important when preparing and storing data, otherwise it can be a total nightmare when you need to find the data again. Finding data after it's been stored is called data retrieval.

Using an Organised Filing System is Best

In the workplace, a lot of time can be wasted looking for where data is stored. To avoid this businesses set up filing systems. There are two types — manual and electronic.

Manual Filing Systems

1) Manual systems are paper based. Files can be organised so they are sorted by letters of the alphabet — called an alphabetic system. Or they can be sorted numerically — by number. Or they can be stored in date order — this is called chronological order.

2) The type of system used will depend on the kind of data being kept. If the system is storing data on people or other businesses then an alphabetical system is more likely to be used. Data on products or invoices is usually filed numerically.

Electronic Filing Systems

1) When data is stored on a computer it will be stored in a computer file — this is electronic filing. The files are also stored alphabetically or numerically.

2) Computer files are organised into folders. The folders are the equivalent of a filing cabinet drawer in manual systems. Each folder may be given a name that helps describe the type of data stored.

Manual and Electronic Systems Have Different Benefits

1) The main advantage of a manual filing system is that it is simple to understand.

2) The main disadvantage of a manual system is that a lot of space is needed to store files. Also there can be problems of misfiling or files being taken and not being returned.

3) An advantage of electronic filing is that it saves on office space as no filing cabinets are needed. Retrieval is quicker so long as users are well trained in how the system works.

4) A disadvantage of electronic filing is if the computer system fails the files cannot be retrieved.

Keeping Files Safe is Important for Businesses

1) Keeping data safe is essential because it can contain important information like customer details and financial information. Businesses need to make sure that they are kept safe in case of fire, theft and flood. They do this by storing manual files in fire and water proof cabinets.

2) Computer files are backed up (copied) regularly. All back-up copies are kept on disk or tape. These should be stored off site or in fire and water proof cabinets.

3) If files need to be kept in the long term but aren't frequently used, (e.g. former employee details or tax files) then they are archived — kept in a different place from the main system. This stops the main system of short-term files becoming over loaded.

I prefer to file my nails...

Some filing systems will use revision control, so each time a file is updated or changed a number or letter code will be added to the file name so you can see which is the most recent file.

SECTION TWO — WORKPLACE ORGANISATION & DATA MANAGEMENT

Security — Networks

There are three main types of network security: physical security, access security and data security.

Physical Security Protects the Hardware

Hardware is expensive — to keep it safe these 6 rules need to be followed.

1) **Serial numbers** — Keep a record of all serial numbers, and mark the organisation's name and postcode on all equipment — this helps police to identify stolen property.
2) **Alarms** — Computer rooms should be protected by burglar alarms.
3) **Fire protection** — Use fireproof doors and smoke alarms. Also, automatic gas-flooding systems could be used to put out any fire to prevent water damaging the equipment.
4) **Lock** windows and doors to prevent access.
5) **Avoid** putting computers where they can be easily seen from outside, where possible.
6) **Blinds** or curtains should be closed at night, and monitors should be switched off, so the computers are less visible.

Access Security Limits a Person's Use of the Network

1) All authorised users should be given user names and create their own passwords. This will limit unauthorised access to the network.
2) Users should change their password frequently.
3) Individual users can be assigned access rights — for example network managers can be given access to the software that controls how the network is run. Other users can be limited to certain types of applications software such as word processors.
4) The network can be protected from external threats (like hackers) by using a firewall.
5) Transaction logs are files that record every change made to a document. This means you can find previous versions of the document or even the master if you want to.

Data Security Prevents Loss of Data

1) Some software and files can be password-protected so that a password is needed to view and amend data.
2) Files can be made read-only, so that they cannot be altered or deleted. Other files may be hidden so that they are not visible to the user.
3) Regular back-ups should be made of the data on the system using suitable backing storage. The main method used to back-up network data is the ancestral method.
4) Back-up files should be kept secure — ideally in locked fireproof rooms in a different location to the network.
5) Files are often compressed (reduced in size) when they are backed up in order to save space.

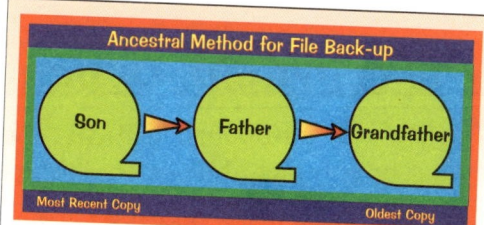
Ancestral Method for File Back-up
Son → Father → Grandfather
Most Recent Copy / Oldest Copy

The son is the most recent copy of the file. When the next back-up is made, this becomes the father. When the next back-up is made the father becomes the grandfather. The grandfather file is deleted when a new son is created.
If the original file is lost or damaged there are three back-up files available.

Making three copies of everything would get my back-up...

Most of this is common sense — especially if you think about how a school computer network operates. Write out all the information until you've memorised every single little bit of it.

SECTION TWO — WORKPLACE ORGANISATION & DATA MANAGEMENT

Security — Hackers, Viruses and Copyright

Businesses need to protect their data and networks from risks like hackers and viruses. There are also laws that set out rules for businesses on protecting certain data and ideas.

Protection from Hackers and Viruses is needed

1) Hacking means accessing a computer system and its files without permission. It's totally illegal, and once inside a system, the hacker might be able to view, edit, copy or delete important files, or plant a virus. Businesses can protect themselves by using passwords, encrypting files and using hacking-detection software.

2) A virus is a program deliberately written to infect a computer, and make copies of itself. They often corrupt other files — and even operating systems. They move between computer systems by attaching themselves to harmless computer files and e-mails.

3) The main way to reduce the risk of viruses is to use anti-virus software — but it's important to use an up-to-date version because new viruses are detected practically every day.

The Computer Misuse Act prevents Illegal Access to Files

This law was introduced in 1990 to cope with the problems of computer hackers and viruses. The Act made the following three things illegal:

1) Unauthorised access to computer material (e.g. hacking). This includes viewing parts of a network you're not permitted to see, and the illegal copying of programs — software piracy.

2) Gaining unauthorised access to a computer to carry out serious crimes like fraud and blackmail.

3) Unauthorised changing of computer files — including planting viruses and deleting files.

If convicted, the offender can face an unlimited fine and a five-year prison sentence.

The Copyright, Design & Patents Act controls Illegal Copying

This law was introduced in 1989, and makes it illegal to copy a file without permission from the owner or copyright holder. Individuals and businesses who break this law risk an unlimited fine.

There are three ways that the law is often broken:

1) Using software without the proper licence. So if you have a licence to use a word processor on one stand-alone computer, but you then install it on all the machines in a network, you're breaking the law.

2) Downloading text or images from the Internet and using them without saying where you got them, or without receiving the copyright owner's permission.

3) Copying a computer program you use at work and running it on a computer at home, without permission from the copyright holder.

Piracy — not such a fun job without treasure and a parrot...

Most people know someone who knows someone who can get their hands on the latest films before they hit the cinema. But the two little laws covered on this page make this illegal.

SECTION TWO — WORKPLACE ORGANISATION & DATA MANAGEMENT

Security — Data Protection

Businesses and other organisations keep data on customers, patients, students and individuals — whether on paper or on computer files. There are laws to control how the data is used.

The Data Protection Act Controls How Data is Kept and Used

1) According to the Data Protection Act (1998) any business or organisation that holds personal data about individuals must register with the Registrar of Data Protection.
2) The act covers all data — both paper records and electronically stored data.

There are Eight Principles of Data Protection

1. Data must not be processed unless there is a specific lawful reason to do so — such as checking whether a person has a good record of paying back money borrowed on credit cards.
2. Data can only be obtained and used for specified purposes. E.g. businesses may need to have names and addresses to deliver goods. If they want to use the data for advertising in the future, they have to ask the data subject's permission.
3. Data should be adequate, relevant and not excessive for the specified use. E.g. if a business is collecting data to deliver goods to you, they shouldn't ask for your national insurance number.
4. Data must be accurate and kept up to date. For example, a student's examination results must be updated each time they sit additional exams. If this didn't happen, incorrect information could be given in a reference to another college or potential employer.
5. Data should not be kept longer than is necessary for the specified purpose. This depends on why the data is being kept — financial information can be kept for up to seven years, but medical records are kept for the life of a patient.
6. Data processing should meet the legal rights of the data subjects by keeping some information confidential. No business can pass bank details on without the permission of the data subject.
7. Data holders must protect the data against loss, theft or corruption. The duty is on the holders to back up data and to dispose of it properly.
8. Data should not be transferred abroad, except to certain other European countries. This is to protect people from businesses who may try to do this so that they can avoid UK law.

Organisations that break the law can be fined and could be made to pay compensation to the data subject.

The Data Protection Act (1998) gives these rights to data subjects:

1) The right to view data held about them (but they must give notice and maybe pay a small fee).
2) The right to prevent the processing of data that might cause distress or damage to themselves.
3) The right to compensation if damage or distress has been caused.
4) The right to have any inaccurate data changed or deleted.
5) The right to prevent data being used to send junk mail.

There are Some Exceptions to the Law

Data that is used for national security purposes is not subject to the principles of the Data Protection Act. Personal data that is used to help prevent or solve crime, prosecute criminals or for tax assessment purposes is also exempt from some of the data protection principles.

Data Protection — easier than 'gator protection...

The Data Protection Act means businesses have to protect your data — so David Beckham's bank can't tell us how much he spends on hair gel a month, unless it was a case of national security...

SECTION TWO — WORKPLACE ORGANISATION & DATA MANAGEMENT

Efficiency of Systems

A <u>business system</u> is the <u>process</u> a business uses to get something done. Business systems can include electronic data processing, making a product or passing on communications.

Any System is Only as Good as the Staff who Use it

Staff involved in a system have to have the skills and knowledge to make it work <u>efficiently</u>. There are a number of different factors that affect how well staff can use systems:

1) How <u>motivated</u> staff are can affect how well the system works. Some systems make jobs <u>less interesting</u>. They have precise instructions and staff can't use their initiative, which is demotivating. Modern systems are designed to <u>work faster</u>, which can lead to <u>job losses</u> — this could <u>demotivate</u> remaining staff, affecting the quality of their work.

2) If staff have to <u>learn new skills</u> to use a system, the skills might be <u>difficult</u> to learn, or staff might <u>resist</u> the changes because they don't like them. Until the skills of the staff are up to scratch the new system won't work efficiently.

3) <u>Information flow</u> between staff in a system needs to be clear. For example, notes made on customers' records must be clearly worded and passed on to other staff that need them.

4) <u>Working conditions</u> can affect how efficiently systems work. Staff can <u>lose concentration</u> if they can't take breaks or are uncomfortable. This causes mistakes to be made.

Any System is only as Good as the Equipment Used

1) For a system to work efficiently, the business needs to buy the <u>right equipment</u> to do the job. Most large business employ <u>experts</u> to <u>design the system</u> and <u>install the equipment</u> needed.

2) Equipment and software must be <u>reliable</u> and <u>easy to maintain</u>. If the system goes 'offline' — that is breaks down — the business might lose production time or customer orders. Some businesses may have a back up system which will kick in if the main system goes 'offline'.

This is our new state of the art word processing system.

3) Instead of buying whole new systems some businesses <u>upgrade systems</u> to take advantage of <u>new technology</u> or <u>processes</u>. This means that modern parts or the latest version software is used to replace older versions. By law all <u>old computer equipment</u> must be <u>disposed</u> of by <u>specialist companies</u>.

4) Sometimes dealing with <u>environmental issues</u>, like waste disposal, can affect how the business's systems work. For example, if a business has to dispose of hazardous chemicals used in its production process, it will have to pay for them to be reprocessed or disposed of appropriately — this makes the system more costly.

Efficient ICT Systems Can Give a Competitive Edge

Customers want to deal with <u>efficient businesses</u>. Those that can provide this type of service will be able to beat the competition and be more <u>profitable</u>. If they have good ICT systems and well trained staff they can gain more <u>market share</u>.

The competitive Edge — when he plays conkers with Bono...

Every part of a system needs to work well together for things to be efficient. Make sure you know how both employees and equipment can affect how the system works...

SECTION TWO — WORKPLACE ORGANISATION & DATA MANAGEMENT

Revision Summary for Section Two

Well, there was a bit more stuff here than in Section 1. Unfortunately those odd examiners are impressed by facts so you need to know everything. Use the questions below to prove that you are a master mind of data management and workplace organisation. Once you can answer all these questions you'll be rewarded by the whole of the next section not having any Star Trek gags.

1) What is job sharing?
2) Give two advantages of job sharing to employees.
3) What is flexitime?
4) Name two advantages for a business of having multi-skilled employees.
5) What is hot desking?
6) Why do some businesses choose to use external specialists or consultants?
7) How are open plan offices arranged?
8) List two disadvantages of cellular offices.
9) Why do businesses give their staff ergonomically designed furniture?
10) Which of the following is true about call centre opening hours?
    a) They are only open on the third Monday of every month.
    b) They are usually open longer than normal business hours.
    c) They are only open when businesses are closed for lunch.
11) Give two reasons why some customers don't like call centres.
12) Which two health and safety laws do employers have to comply with?
13) Name the three main health problems using computers can cause.
14) What is a data capture form?
15) How do EPOS and bar codes work?
16) What is EFTPOS?
17) Name the four types of computer application that can be used to record data.
18) Give two factors that affect how data is presented.
19) What are the four different ways data can be presented?
20) Why is it important to spend preparation time making sure a presentation is clear and accurate?
21) What is a manual filing system?
22) List two advantages of using an electronic filing system.
23) Why is it important for businesses to keep their data safe?
24) List the six rules businesses should follow to protect their hardware.
25) Explain how the ancestral back-up system works.
26) What is a virus?
27) What three things does the Computer Misuse Act make illegal?
28) What does the Copyright, Design and Patents Act make illegal?
29) List the eight principles of data protection.
30) Give two examples of when the Data Protection Act doesn't have to be complied with.
31) Describe three factors which affect how well staff can use systems.

SECTION TWO — WORKPLACE ORGANISATION & DATA MANAGEMENT

Recruitment — Job Analysis

This section is all about people in the workplace which is called human resources (HR). The human resource cycle looks after the different stages of an individual's employment — recruitment and selection, induction, training, performance, appraisal, development and departure. This page is only for students studying the AQA syllabus (check with your teacher if you're not sure which syllabus you're doing).

The Job Description Says What the Job Is

1) The job description is a written description of what the job consists of. It includes the formal title of the job, its main purpose, its main duties and any occasional duties.

2) It will also include details of who the job holder is responsible to and whether they are responsible for managing other staff. It may include some performance targets.

3) Without a job description it would be impossible to write the person specification.

Count Dracula Vampires Ltd. — Job Description
Job Title: Junior Vampire.
Location: St Peter's Graveyard.
Purpose: To climb through people's windows at night and generally act in a scary way.
Activities:
— to work between the hours of dusk and dawn biting the necks of people whilst they sleep;
— to wear a large black cape and laugh in a scary way;
— to meet neck biting targets set by the Senior Vampire.
Responsible to: Senior Vampire.

The Person Specification Describes the Ideal Person

Junior Vampire — Person Specification
Essential: 5 GCSEs including Business Studies, NVQ Vampiring Level 3.
Desirable: Two years vampiring experience.
Skills: Ability to climb through windows, bite necks, turn into a bat and fly off. Good communication skills.
Personal qualities: Scary face, large incisor teeth, must not like daylight, must enjoy meeting new people.

1) The person specification lists the qualifications, experience, skills and personal qualities of the ideal candidate.

2) They are sometimes divided into essential criteria, which the right candidate must have, and desirable criteria — which the right candidate should have.

The Job Advertisement Gets People to Apply

Before they advertise a job, a firm might try to fill the vacancy with someone personally recommended by an existing worker. This can be cheaper and less hassle than advertising.

1) The purpose of a job advert is to get as many suitable people as possible to apply for the job. The firm should decide what it should contain, where it will be put and for how long.

2) A firm might decide to advertise internally. Adverts are usually put up on noticeboards or sent round to staff. Advantages of recruiting internally are that it is much cheaper and the post can be filled more quickly. Also the candidates will already know a lot about the firm and its objectives. On the downside, there will be no 'new blood' and ideas, and the promotion will leave another vacancy to fill.

3) If the job is advertised externally, the firm has to decide where to advertise. Locations include local and national press, job centres, the internet, trade journals or periodicals and employment agencies. Only specialist and senior jobs get advertised in the national press — because it's very expensive. Advertising jobs externally means the business can bring in people with new ideas and new skills.

4) The advert should describe the job and the skills required. It will often indicate what the pay is, and what training and other benefits are offered. It must explain how the person should apply for the job.

Person specification — a chance to describe your ideal man...

Hmmm... tall, dashing, rich... I'd settle for Keanu Reeves, Jake Gyllenhaal, George Clooney, Orlando Bloom or Johnny Depp. Oh, sorry — got a bit distracted there. Right, back to BCS...

Recruitment — The Selection Process

The selection process happens after the job has been advertised. All the applications are looked at and employers create a shortlist of people to interview. This page is just for AQA students.

Written Applications Help the Firm to Make a Shortlist

The written application enables the business to decide which candidates meet the person specification — and which don't. There are three kinds of written application.

1) In a letter of application the candidates write about themselves — it gives the business an idea of the applicant's personality as well as their written communication skills.

2) A curriculum vitae (CV) is a summary of a person's personal details, skills, qualifications and interests. It is written in a standard format to give the business the basic facts.

3) An application form is designed by the business and completed by the applicant. It gives the business the information that it wants — and nothing else.

Shortlisted candidates will have their references checked. These are statements about the character of the candidate written by someone who knows them — often their line manager. They are usually confidential — the candidate will not see what is written about them.

Most businesses now accept electronic versions of written applications. Some even have online application forms.

A good application will be to the point and refer to skills and qualities mentioned in the job description and person specification.

A bad application might be waffly, not contain enough information or be poorly written.

Shortlisted Candidates are Interviewed

The interviewer and the interviewee both have to prepare for the interview.

INTERVIEWER PREPARATION
1) Find somewhere suitable to carry out the interview.
2) Write a list of interview questions. The same questions should be asked to all candidates to make the interview fair.
3) Read through the interviewee's application again.
4) Write any tests the interviewees will be asked to do.

INTERVIEWEE PREPARATION
1) Read the job description and person specification again.
2) Find out about the business.
3) Dress smartly.
4) Think of examples to use in their answers.

Interviews can be Formal or Informal

1) In formal interview situations the room is laid out with the interviewer(s) sitting behind a table with the candidate facing them. The interviewer will ask set questions and will make notes or give marks for the answers given.

2) Informal interviews are more casual where interviews may arrange the room in such a way that the interview takes the form of a conversation. Candidates will be more relaxed and can show their personalities. The interviewer may still make notes or complete a check list.

Sorry, I can never behave naturally at interviews.

Shortlisting — arranging candidates in height order...

Nothing too tricky here — cover up the page and scribble down the preparation the interviewer needs to do before an interview. Then scribble down how an interviewee needs to prepare.

SECTION THREE — HUMAN RESOURCES

Recruitment — Starting & Ending Contracts

To protect both the employees and business there has to be a contract of employment. Businesses also have disciplinary procedures so they can tackle employees who do not behave appropriately. This page is just for AQA students.

At the Start of a Job You Get a Contract of Employment

A contract of employment can be verbal or written. It is a legal agreement between the employee and the employer.

It will tell the employee:

1) The hours they have to work.
2) Their starting pay and the regular date of payment.
3) The number of days holidays they are entitled to.
4) If they are entitled to sickness pay.
5) Notice of termination of employment the employee has to give the employer.
6) The starting date of the employment.
7) The job title or a brief job description.
8) Information on any pension scheme available to employees through the employer.

Employers or Employees can Terminate Contracts of Employment

The employer can terminate a contract for the following reasons:

1) **Redundancy** — when the business reorganises or the job position is no longer needed. If made redundant then employees are entitled to redundancy pay. To get redundancy pay they must be over 18 and have worked for the company for over a year.
2) **Dismissal** — employees can be dismissed from their jobs if they break their contract of employment, e.g. bad time-keeping, frequent absences from work, poor performance or if they commit an action the business thinks is gross misconduct.

An employee can terminate the contract when they:

1) **Resign** — an employee can leave their job by giving the amount of notice stated in their contract, usually a week or a month.
2) **Retire** — when an employee decides to finish their working life, usually when they are 60 or 65. It is becoming more popular to take early retirement.

Early retirement was a great idea.

All Businesses Have Disciplinary Procedures

1) These will include procedures for giving warnings before dismissal. There are two types of warnings — informal and formal.
2) Informal warnings are given by a manager or supervisor. They're usually verbal. If the employee's behaviour does not improve then a formal, written warning may be given. After three formal warnings have been issued an employee can be dismissed if their behaviour does not improve.
3) Gross misconduct is an action for which employees can be dismissed without notice — e.g. if an employee commits theft, endangers other workers or comes to work drunk.

Ex-terminate, ex-terminate the contract...

You need to know what has to be included in the contract of employment — so cover up the page and jot down all 8 points. If you don't get them all read the page again and give it another go.

SECTION THREE — HUMAN RESOURCES

Employment and the Law

There are loads of laws designed to look after employees, while also recognising the needs of businesses. They make sure businesses treat all staff equally.

Some Laws Affect Recruitment and Contracts of Employment

1) Recruitment procedures must not discriminate against women, ethnic minorities or the disabled. This is covered by the Sex Discrimination Act 1975, the Race Relations Act 1976 and the Disability Discrimination Act 1995.

2) All employees must receive a written contract of employment within one month of starting work. This is covered by the Employment Rights Act 1996.

3) All employers must provide a disciplinary procedure for all employees. Minor problems may receive a verbal or written warning. More serious offences that are grounds for instant dismissal will be listed. This is covered by the Employment Protection Act of 1975.

4) The Government sets a National Minimum Wage for all workers. In October 2005 it was £4.25/hour for 18-21 year-olds, £5.05/hour if you're over 22. The amount is regularly increased, in October 2006 it will rise to £4.45/hour for 18-21 year-olds, £5.35/hour if you're over 22.

5) Women have the right to maternity leave of up to 52 weeks and will be able to keep their job with the company. For the first six weeks of maternity leave they will get 90% of their normal pay and then £108.85 (or 90% of their pay, whichever is less) per week for the next 20 weeks. Fathers are allowed two weeks of paternity leave.

Other Laws Prevent Discrimination

1) Apart from recruitment the other main equal opportunities issue is pay. The 1970 Equal Pay Act says that an employee must be paid the same as another employee doing the same job. The act was intended to give men and women equal pay.

2) Men and women often do different jobs — so exact pay comparisons are difficult. The 1983 Equal Pay Act made it compulsory to give the same pay for work of equal value. So a midwife supervisor should be paid the same as other equivalent managerial jobs.

3) It is also illegal to discriminate against employees with disabilities or against employees from ethnic minorities. There are laws that prevent discrimination in terms of pay, contracts of employment, conditions of work, training or promotions.

The European Union can Affect Employment Law

When the EU passes directives, countries that belong to the EU agree to make the directive into law in their country. The EU Working Time Directive 1998 is a good example.

EU Working Time Directive

This sets out rules on working hours and holidays.
1) The working week is limited to 48 hours.
2) Night shifts should not be more than 8 hours in each 24 hour period.
3) Every employee is entitled to a 20 minute break if the working day is longer than 6 hours.
4) Employees have to be given a minimum of four weeks' paid holiday a year.

Employment rights — better than employment wrongs...

There are lots of laws on this page that you need to know. Make sure you learn when they were passed and how they affect both the employees and the business.

SECTION THREE — HUMAN RESOURCES

Workplace Policies and Practices

Workplace policies and practices are basically rules that everyone in a business has to follow. They tell employees how they should behave at work. (Students studying the Edexcel syllabus don't need to learn this page. It's just for AQA and OCR students.)

Some Policies are Legal Requirements

Businesses create some policies because they help them comply with laws and EU directives. E.g. policies help businesses comply with the Health and Safety at Work Act 1974. Businesses have to create a safe working environment for their staff. They will have policies on:

There's more about the Health and Safety Act on page 12.

1) Using machinery — All firms will have rules about how machines should be operated, any safety equipment that has to be used, or safety clothing that has to be worn when using machinery.

2) Alcohol and drug abuse — Employees who are under the influence of drink or drugs are a danger to other workers. The use of drugs and alcohol on work premises is usually banned.

3) Emergency procedures — All firms should have policies covering the evacuation of the workplace in case of fire or gas leaks. There should also be procedures in place to help disabled staff or visitors leave the building in an emergency.

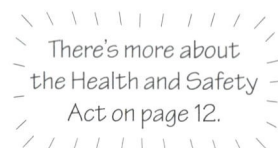

In the event of an emergency — RUN

Others Policies Cover Behaviour and Clothing

Jeff, you can't work on the till dressed like that.

1) Dress codes tell employees what they can or can't wear. It might be for safety reasons or to create a certain corporate image. Many businesses have policies on what employees should wear if they meet clients or the public — often they specify they must wear suits or a company supplied uniform.

2) No smoking policy — most businesses do not allow smoking in the workplace because of the dangers to health from passive smoking. There is also a risk of fire in the workplace.

3) There may also be policies on how telephones are answered or how customers are greeted.

4) Some businesses also have policies to ensure good employee welfare — for example, providing health or childcare benefits, social clubs or subsidised staff canteens.

There are Usually Policies for Consulting with Staff

1) Good employers have consultation procedures for informing and consulting their employees when they plan to make changes in the workplace. There will be policies about how and when staff will be consulted. Staff might be consulted about changes like proposing a new pay structure, working conditions or staff uniform.

2) If most of the workers belong to a trade union then consultation will probably go through the union. There might also be a staff consultation committee who represents the employees during consultations.

3) By law businesses have to have a grievance procedure so that employees can raise problems such as discrimination or bullying by managers or other employees.

Emergency procedures — essential for bad hair days...

Legally businesses must have policies that create a safe working environment and safe working practices and a policy for grievance procedures. Other policies are rules created by the business.

SECTION THREE — HUMAN RESOURCES

Staff Training

Training is the main way that a firm invests in its workers. A well trained workforce will usually be more productive because they're better at their jobs. They might also be better motivated because they enjoy feeling that they're good at what they're doing. Training should start on the very first day. (Students studying Edexcel don't need to learn this page.)

Induction Training is for New Staff

1) Induction training introduces the new employee to their workplace.
2) It includes introducing them to their fellow workers and advising them of company rules — including health and safety rules. They should be given a tour of the site so they don't get lost. It may also include initial training on how to do their new job.
3) It should help to make the new employee feel welcome.

On-the-Job Training is Learning by Doing

1) This is the most common form of training. The person learns to do their job better by being shown how to do it — and then practising. It is also sometimes called internal training.
2) It is cost-effective for the employer because the person continues to work while learning.
3) A problem is that it is often taught by a colleague — so bad working practices can be passed on.

Yeah, we're supposed to lock the safe every night, but we never actually bother.

Off-the-Job Training can be Internal or External

1) This happens when the person learns away from their workplace. Sometimes it is still done internally, if the firm has a separate training division. It is called external training if it happens outside the business — for example at college.
2) It's more expensive than on-the-job training and sometimes not as practical — but it is often of a higher quality because it will be taught by better-qualified people.
3) It is best used when introducing new skills or training people for promotion.

Sometimes Staff Need Retraining

Before you can use the new X900 photocopier you need to memorise this 200000 page manual.

1) Staff appraisals are carried out to check an employee's skills and productivity. A manager can use these to identify if an employee needs some training to improve their skills or increase productivity.
2) When new processes or equipment are introduced staff will need to be retrained.
3) Firms which invest in staff development can gain Investors in People status. This signals that they are good employers — making it easier to recruit staff.

Training — it's like coaching, only it runs on tracks...

There are three different types of training. Make sure you know what each one is and that you can give an advantage and disadvantage for each. Training is good for improving productivity of staff.

SECTION THREE — HUMAN RESOURCES

Financial Rewards

There are a lot of facts on this page but it all boils down to two things — the different ways of paying people and what work incentives each method gives them.

If People Do More Work Their Wages Increase...

Wages are paid weekly or monthly — usually to manual workers. There is a legal minimum wage (see page 27). Wages are calculated in one of two ways.

At this rate I can make this job last all week...

1) A time rate pays workers by the hour. If a painter is paid £6 per hour and works 50 hours in a week, their week's wage is £300. Time rate encourages people to work long hours — the problem is they also have an incentive to work slowly. Time rate is best for jobs where measuring a worker's output is difficult — like driving a bus.

2) A piece rate is used if the output of each worker can be easily measured. If a worker who sews sleeves onto shirts is paid a piece rate of 10p per sleeve and they sew 2000 sleeves in a week then their weekly wage will be £200. Piece rate encourages people to work quickly — the problem is they work so fast that quality may suffer.

What do you mean, it's poor quality work?

...But a Salary Stays the Same

1) A salary is a fixed amount paid every month. It is usually paid to office staff and management who do not directly help to make the product. A salary of £24,000 means you are paid £2000 per month.

2) The advantage of a salary is that the business and workers both know exactly how much the pay will be.

3) A disadvantage is that it does not link pay to performance, so it does not encourage employees to work harder.

Performance-Related Pay Matches Rewards to Quality

Performance-related pay (PRP) is becoming more popular — how much people earn depends on how well they work. There are three main types of PRP.

1) Commission is paid to sales staff. They earn a small basic salary and then earn more money for every item they sell.

2) A bonus is a lump sum added to pay, usually once a year. It is paid if the worker has met their performance targets.

3) Profit-sharing gives each worker an agreed share of company profits. If the company does well, the payment will be bigger.

Please buy some more double glazing — I need the commission to buy a goat shed.

Salary — I like it with lettuce and tomatoes...

Employees can be paid overtime if they work over their contracted number of hours — it doesn't matter if they are paid wages, a salary or if they are on performance-related pay.

SECTION THREE — HUMAN RESOURCES

//
Financial Rewards

Pay isn't the only way to reward employees. There are other ways businesses can reward their staff, to motivate them and make them more productive — these are sometimes called fringe benefits. But before you get to that, you first need to learn how businesses actually pay their staff.

Employers have to make Deductions from Gross Pay

1) Gross pay is the amount of money an employee is paid — their wage or salary. However, the amount that an employee actually gets to keep is called net pay.

2) Net pay is gross pay minus some deductions. Some deductions are compulsory — everyone has to pay income tax and National Insurance contributions. You can also choose to pay voluntary deductions — like pension contributions.

3) PAYE (Pay As You Earn) is where the employer automatically deducts tax from your pay before you receive it.

TD means 'to date'.

DATE	NAME	TAX CODE	N.I. NUMBER	
20/09/06	B. SMART	374L	JB236597	
PAY		DEDUCTIONS		
SALARY	1600	INCOME TAX	280	TOTAL GROSS PAY 1600
		NAT. INS.	115	GROSS FOR TAX TD 7890
		PENSION	50	TAX PAID TD 1350
				N.I. TD 575
				PENSION TD 250
TOTAL	1600	TOTAL	445	NET PAY 1155

4) Pay slips show an employee how much their net pay is and how it's been worked out.

5) Workers can be paid in different ways — cash, cheque or BACS (Bankers Automated Clearing System). BACS is where the employer gets the bank to transfer money directly into your bank account.

Fringe Benefits are Extra Benefits an Employee Gets

Sometimes, in addition to their salary or wages, employees can be given fringe benefits. They can be financial or non-financial. Financial fringe benefits are normally taxable.

FINANCIAL FRINGE BENEFITS
1) Staff discounts
2) Employee pensions
3) Private medical insurance
4) Company car

NON-FINANCIAL FRINGE BENEFITS
1) Praise
2) Training
3) Additional responsibility

Training and Development can be a Reward

1) Training helps employees to be good at their job. It also shows the employee that the business values them and is willing to invest money in them. Training gives workers new skills and makes them more productive. But training can be expensive for businesses to carry out.

2) Job enrichment is when a worker is given greater responsibility — for example supervising the work of new staff. The idea is to give employees new tasks and challenges that they will find rewarding. As a result the employee should be motivated and work harder. A problem for the business of job enrichment is that workers may expect a pay rise as well.

Fringe benefits — free hair cuts...

There's no hiding from all the facts you need to know on this page. Start by seeing if you can list the contributions deducted from pay. Then make a list of all the fringe benefits firms can offer.

SECTION THREE — HUMAN RESOURCES

Revision Summary for Section Three

Phew — you've made it to the end of the human resources section. There's lots to learn, but it should be straightforward. It's really important to learn all the employment laws and how they affect the HR cycle at its different stages. To see how much you've remembered have a go at these questions — and keep going over the section till you're sure you can answer them all.

1) List four things that should be included on a job description.
2) Explain the difference between a job description and a person specification.
3) Give one advantage and one disadvantage of advertising a job internally.
4) What information should the job advert include?
5) What are the three types of written application?
6) List four things an interviewer has to do to prepare for an interview.
7) What should an interviewee do to prepare for an interview?
   a) write a CV   b) find out about the business   c) dress like a clown
8) List eight points the contract of employment should include.
9) What are the two ways an employer can terminate a contract?
10) How can an employee terminate a contract of employment?
11) What are the two types of disciplinary warning that can be given to an employee?
12) What three laws protect employees against discrimination?
13) What must all employees be given within one month of starting work?
    a) a contract   b) a pay rise   c) the sack
14) What did the Equal Pay Acts of 1970 and 1983 make law?
15) How many hours does the EU Working Time Directive limit the working week to?
16) List five workplace policies a business might have.
17) Why might a business have a dress code?
18) What should happen during induction training?
19) Explain the difference between on-the-job and off-the-job training.
20) Give one advantage and one disadvantage of on-the-job training.
21) What do you call the pay method when workers are paid by the hour?
22) Explain one problem with the piece rate pay method.
23) What is an advantage of paying staff a salary?
24) Explain the three kinds of performance-related pay.
25) Name two compulsory deductions from pay.
26) What is PAYE?
27) What three ways can employees be paid?
28) List six fringe benefits.

SECTION FOUR — COMMUNICATION

Purposes of Communication

It's really important that businesses can get their message across to customers and other important folk. Businesses may as well not bother existing if they can't tell anybody what they're up to.

Communication Involves the Exchange of Information

1) Here's a nice definition of communication for you: "Communication is when a person or a group exchanges information with another person or group."
2) Information messages can be communicated through different channels (also called mediums) e.g. emails, meetings, letters, phone calls.
3) The person who receives the message can give feedback to show they've understood it.

Businesses Communicate Internally and Externally

Internal communication (between people inside the business)

Good internal communication is important for the smooth running of the business, e.g.
1) Managers and supervisors need to communicate with operatives to tell them what to do.
2) Departments need to communicate with other departments within the business to find out information or co-ordinate activities.
3) The business objectives and targets need to be communicated to all employees.
4) Shareholders need to be given information about how the business is performing. E.g. they need to see profit and loss accounts and be told whether objectives are being met.

External communication (with people outside the business)

Good communication with external stakeholders is also important, e.g.
1) Businesses need to communicate with their suppliers to agree the size, cost and delivery dates of orders.
2) Businesses need to communicate with their customers in order to improve sales, e.g. market research to find out what customers want, and advertising to promote their products.
3) Businesses also communicate with customers through customer care — e.g. dealing with complaints and queries about products.
4) Customers can communicate with the business by giving customer feedback.

Effective Communication Helps Achieve Objectives

1) Businesses with good external communications are more likely to know what products to make and how to sell them profitably. If businesses listen to their customers through customer feedback, they will understand their needs and so are more likely to meet those needs.
2) Businesses with good internal communications are more likely to have the different divisions in the organisation working well together. The firm will be more likely to produce its products profitably and on time and achieve the business objectives it sets itself.

Talking to a brick wall doesn't count...

Remember that communication is a two-way thing. It's not just about the business telling customers about its products — it's also about it asking the customers for their opinions. Also remember that communication is just as important inside the business as outside. Got that? Good.

Communication Channels

You need to know about the different methods of business communication. Here goes...

Communication is a Two-Way Process

1) Effective communication requires feedback confirming that the message has been understood.

2) One-way communication, which means there is no feedback, runs the risk that the message will be misunderstood by the receiver.

Use the Right Method of Communication for the Message

There are three main methods — written, verbal and visual.

1) **WRITTEN** methods include letters, e-mails, faxes (mainly to people outside the business), and messages on notice boards, memos and reports (mainly to people inside the business).

Written methods are good if a permanent record of the message is needed. The reader can study complex information again and again. Copies can be seen by many people.	But feedback can be difficult to obtain. And if you don't understand what someone has written, it can be hard to check it with them.

2) **VERBAL** methods include telephone calls, one-to-one conversations, group meetings in person or group meetings through video-conferencing.

Verbal methods are good in that information can be given quickly. Body language and tone of voice can reinforce the message and feedback can be easily obtained.	But there is no permanent record of the message and sometimes people forget what they have been told.

3) **VISUAL** methods include films, posters, diagrams and charts. Watching body language is a very powerful way of obtaining non-verbal information from people.

Visual methods are good because complicated information can be summarised so the message is received quickly. Pictures can also communicate feelings and emotions better than words.	But people will interpret images in different ways. Some people find complicated diagrams hard to understand.

ICT is Really Important for Communication

These days most businesses rely on ICT for their communication. Email, telephone, video-conferences, intranets and the internet, for example, are all ICT-dependent methods of communication. There's more about email and the internet on page 41.

Com.. mu..nic... — no, sorry, can't read it...

Can you remember the days before the internet and email? I can't believe people used to actually write each other letters, with pens, and then put them in post boxes. Imagine... how very strange.

SECTION FOUR — COMMUNICATION

Communication — Networks and Hierarchies

A formal communication channel is the official way communication takes place in a firm.
You need to know how different organisation structures affect how communication takes place.

A Long Chain of Command is a Problem

1) Communication up and down the hierarchy is called vertical communication. Dodgy Computers has six levels in its hierarchy — so its chain of command has six layers.

2) A long chain of command is bad because messages take a long time to travel up and down the hierarchy. People at each end feel isolated from the other end. This can result in poor morale. Messages might not reach the other end and if they do they might get distorted along the way — rather like a game of Chinese whispers.

3) Some firms have tried to solve the problem of a long chain of command by de-layering — removing tiers of management, usually in the middle.

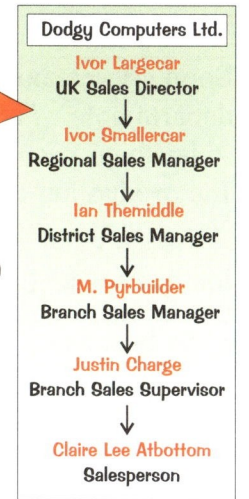

Dodgy Computers Ltd.
Ivor Largecar — UK Sales Director
↓
Ivor Smallercar — Regional Sales Manager
↓
Ian Themiddle — District Sales Manager
↓
M. Pyrbuilder — Branch Sales Manager
↓
Justin Charge — Branch Sales Supervisor
↓
Claire Lee Atbottom — Salesperson

A Wide Span of Control is also a Problem

1) Communication along the same level in the hierarchy is called horizontal or lateral communication. The manager of Clevercloggs Software has a span of control of nine workers.

2) Horizontal communication can cause problems if one person has to give messages to lots of others — it can take time and people may feel that they lack personal contact.

3) Firms must find the right balance between a small chain of command and a narrow span of control.

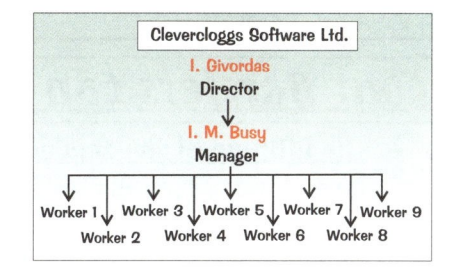

Clevercloggs Software Ltd.
I. Givordas — Director
↓
I. M. Busy — Manager
↓
Worker 1, Worker 2, Worker 3, Worker 4, Worker 5, Worker 6, Worker 7, Worker 8, Worker 9

The Right Communication Network can Help

1) Horizontal and vertical communication are two examples of a chain network. Two alternatives are the wheel network and the connected network.

2) The wheel has a key person at the centre who communicates directly with all other parts. It's good for solving problems but is bad because different parts of the network can't speak to each other.

3) The connected network is where everyone communicates with everyone else. It's good for exchanging ideas between different groups in the firm, but is bad for decision-making because there's no one in overall control.

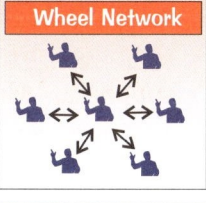

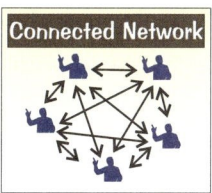

Wheel Network

Connected Network

Good Informal Communication Channels can also Help

1) Informal communication channels are often called the grapevine. Messages get passed by word of mouth between colleagues throughout the firm. Information gets passed quickly this way.

2) The problem is that rumours and disinformation also get spread. Some people might not receive the correct messages and managers are not in control of what information is shared.

I heard it on the grapevine...

So basically, it's really hard getting communication right in a business. There's always someone who feels like they're the last to know about things, or the wrong message gets out. Ho-hum.

SECTION FOUR — COMMUNICATION

Good and Bad Communication — The Effects

Here's a whole page to tell you why good communication is good for business.

Good Communication Increases Productivity and Profit

Inside the business

1) Good internal communication helps businesses to co-ordinate activities well between different departments. For example, the sales department communicates with the production department to let them know how many orders have been placed and when the customers expect delivery. The production department then knows how much to produce and by what date.

2) If there's good internal communication, staff will be better informed about what's going on in the business. This should motivate staff, which means they're likely to work harder.

Outside the business

1) Having good external communication often leads to greater customer satisfaction. This is because customers are likely to feel that they've received a good service if they've been kept informed. Customer satisfaction means that customers are more likely to place repeat orders.

2) Part of good communication with customers is using marketing materials effectively. Good marketing materials help create and maintain customer interest and awareness of products.

3) These benefits mean that the business is more likely to run efficiently and make more profit.

Four Barriers Can Prevent Good Communication

① The attitude of the sender or receiver — The sender or receiver might not agree with what's being said, which can affect how the communication is given or understood. Also, if the two people don't get on with each other, the message could get taken the wrong way.

② Organisational problems — In very hierarchical businesses the chain of command can be so long that messages sent by senior managers are not received by operatives. Sometimes the leadership style is autocratic, so workers don't feel encouraged to communicate ideas.

③ Language problems — Language can be an issue when dealing with foreign customers or suppliers. Messages might get mistranslated or cultural differences might not be understood. Jargon is also a problem — the receiver might not understand all the technical terms being used.

④ Management problems — The sender might not have the skills to send the communication clearly or the receiver might not have the skills to understand the communication properly. Messages might be sent to the wrong people. Training can be used to fix this.

Poor Communication Causes Problems

If there is poor internal communication employees may not understand what is going on inside the business. They might feel that their opinion isn't valued if it is misunderstood or ignored. As a result they might feel frustrated and demotivated — so they work less hard as a result.

Poor external communication can give a business a poor image. Customers and suppliers could get dissatisfied if they have a poor relationship with the business. If the business doesn't listen to its customers, it might not get accurate feedback or it could miss out on new business opportunities.

Thumping people you don't like = bad communication...

Poor communication can have a big impact on the business — inefficient, badly-motivated employees and dissatisfied customers are likely to result in fewer sales, less profit and staff leaving.

SECTION FOUR — COMMUNICATION

Written Communication

The next four pages cover the main methods of written communication used by businesses. Your rollercoaster ride into the world of written communication starts with business letters.

Business Letters are Used for External Communication

Letters are one of the main ways in which businesses communicate externally, and are often used for formal internal communication as well. They are used when:
- a formal message needs to be given, e.g. a letter accepting an employee's resignation.
- a permanent record of the message is needed, e.g. a letter confirming changes to a contract.
- a message is complicated or a lot of information needs to be given, e.g. a letter giving feedback to a supplier about goods received.

Business Letters Need to Follow a Standard Layout

The letter below is laid out in a correct business format known as 'fully blocked with open punctuation'.

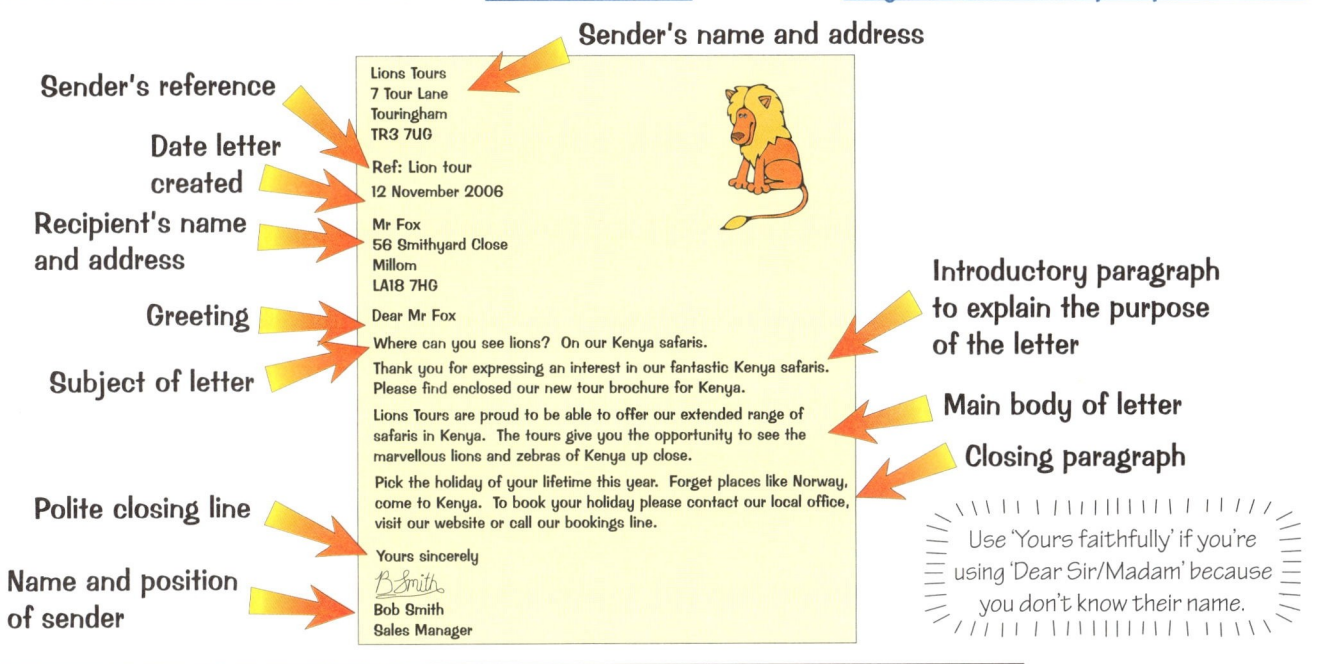

Labels pointing to the example letter:
- Sender's reference
- Date letter created
- Recipient's name and address
- Greeting
- Subject of letter
- Polite closing line
- Name and position of sender
- Sender's name and address
- Introductory paragraph to explain the purpose of the letter
- Main body of letter
- Closing paragraph

Example letter:
Lions Tours
7 Tour Lane
Touringham
TR3 7UG

Ref: Lion tour
12 November 2006

Mr Fox
56 Smithyard Close
Millom
LA18 7HG

Dear Mr Fox

Where can you see lions? On our Kenya safaris.

Thank you for expressing an interest in our fantastic Kenya safaris. Please find enclosed our new tour brochure for Kenya.

Lions Tours are proud to be able to offer our extended range of safaris in Kenya. The tours give you the opportunity to see the marvellous lions and zebras of Kenya up close.

Pick the holiday of your lifetime this year. Forget places like Norway, come to Kenya. To book your holiday please contact our local office, visit our website or call our bookings line.

Yours sincerely
B Smith
Bob Smith
Sales Manager

Use 'Yours faithfully' if you're using 'Dear Sir/Madam' because you don't know their name.

Sending a Letter has Benefits and Drawbacks

Benefits of business letters
1) The business has proof that the message has been sent and of what the message said.
2) Both the sender and receiver can keep the letter and use it for future reference. This can be helpful if the information is important or complicated.
3) The business can have proof that the message was delivered if they use recorded delivery.

Drawbacks of business letters
1) Letters take at least a day to be delivered — so they're not suitable for urgent messages.
2) The sender gets no immediate feedback from the reader, so the sender won't know if the reader has understood the message.

Business — a mail-dominated world...

Business letters are a favourite with examiners, so get this stuff learnt. You'll probably be asked to create your own business letters in your coursework or your exam. Which will be great fun. (ahem)

SECTION FOUR — COMMUNICATION

Written Communication

Although meetings in a business are an example of verbal communication (see pages 44 and 45), a number of written documents need to be produced before and after the meeting.

A Notice of Meeting Invites the Participants to Attend

1) A notice of meeting is sent to all the people who are invited to the meeting. Enough notice should be given so that people are able to attend — two or three weeks should be enough but more might be needed.

2) A notice of meeting should include the name of the person being invited, the date and time of the meeting, where the meeting is being held and what the meeting is about.

3) A notice of meeting is usually sent as a letter or email.

The Agenda Sets Out What Will Happen

The agenda sets out what will be discussed at the meeting and in what order. A set amount of time is sometimes given to each item on the agenda.

Standard Items on an Agenda

1) Apologies for absence — a list of people who were meant to attend the meeting but couldn't.

2) Minutes of the previous meeting. In the meeting, this is where people discuss the previous meeting's minutes (see below) and correct any inaccuracies.

3) Matters arising from the minutes. This is where people report back on any action points from the previous meeting.

4) Correspondence — a list of letters sent and received that will be discussed.

5) The main business of the meeting.

6) Any other business (AOB). This gives people in the meeting an opportunity to discuss issues that were not part of the main agenda.

7) Details of next meeting — can be left vague, to be discussed at the meeting OR if the details are known beforehand, the date, time and venue can be stated here.

The notice of meeting and the agenda are usually published in the same document — the notice goes at the top of the page.

Minutes are a Written Record of the Meeting

1) The minutes of a meeting are a formal record of the meeting. They should record who was there, what was discussed, what decisions where made and if any action points were given. They are best written by someone who was at the meeting.

2) It is important that minutes are accurate because they can be used as proof of what was discussed and agreed.

It only takes a minute girl (to fall in love)...

Chopin's Minute Waltz lasts about three minutes. Radio 4's 'Just a Minute' programme lasts for half an hour. It's false advertising like this that keeps making me late for important meetings.

SECTION FOUR — COMMUNICATION

Written Communication

Here are some more examples of business communications — there are plenty of 'em.

Memo is Short for Memorandum

1) A memorandum (or 'memo') is a formal written message sent to people inside the organisation. Memos are usually used to remind staff of a policy or to tell them about an upcoming event.

2) Memos don't need the company letterhead on them.

3) They can be sent to an individual but are more often sent to a group of people.

4) Memos have largely been replaced by email as the main form of internal written communication.

5) The main advantage of memos is that a permanent record can be kept of the message. This means the business can prove that staff have been given the message.

6) The main disadvantage is that there's no guarantee that staff will actually read the memo.

Below is an example of a memo.

> Memo
>
> To: All sales staff
> From: Anna Flower
> Date: 1/10/06
>
> Subject: Monthly sales prize
> Message: As you all know by now, each month the member of staff who sells the most will receive a prize. This month the prize will be a year's supply of custard — you can chose whether it is powdered or tinned.

A memo should say who it's from, who it's to, the date and the message.

Notices are Put Up Where All Employees can Read Them

1) Notices are meant to be read by the whole staff, so they're put in public places where everyone can see them. The staff canteen or a corridor that everyone uses would be good places.

2) Notices are useful for publicising events or changes to company policy.

Advantages of notices
1) Only a few copies need to be made. This saves money and paper.
2) They can be on display for a long time, giving all staff the chance to see them.
3) The staff will probably see the notice many times, so they're more likely to remember the message.

Disadvantages of notices
1) Some staff might not see or read the notice.
2) It's one-way communication. There's no system for ensuring that staff have received and understood the message.
3) They are only suitable for short and simple messages that aren't confidential.

Verbal Messages Sometimes Need Recording

1) If someone can't answer their phone, a colleague should answer it and take a message. It's best to write messages down or they get forgotten.

2) Most businesses have a standard telephone message form like this that you complete if you're taking a message. This makes it more likely that the message is recorded properly and passed to the right person.

3) An advantage of using a message form is that all staff know what information to collect from the caller. The business will then be able to reply to the caller's enquiry more easily.

You've got an exam on this, so you'd better take notice...

So... there are lots of ways of communicating in a business. I think we've established that by now. Just read the next page on written communication, then go and make yourself a nice cup of tea.

SECTION FOUR — COMMUNICATION

Written Communication

Phew — this is the last page on written communication documents, I promise. However, there are quite a few types of documents covered on this page, so you shouldn't go to sleep just yet.

Reports are Written After Investigations

Reports are written whenever somebody has been asked to carry out an investigation of a topic and give detailed advice and recommendations. Businesses use them in many different ways, for example to help decide on new products or changes to company policy.

Written reports should follow a set format. The main sections of a report are shown below:

1) **Title** — the title of the report, fairly obviously. Also includes who it's written by, and their position in the company.
2) **Terms of Reference** — a statement of what the report covers and who asked for it to be written (who commissioned it).
3) **Procedure** — Sometimes called methodology. This is an explanation of how the research was carried out and how the data collected was analysed.
4) **Findings** — A description of what the research discovered, which includes charts, diagrams or summaries of interviews.
5) **Conclusions** — An explanation of what the research findings tell us about the topic being investigated.
6) **Recommendations** — A summary of what action should be taken as a result of the findings.

...the size of the cow's udder representing anticipated profits...

Flowcharts Summarise a Complex Series of Actions

1) Flowcharts (also known as operating systems) are used whenever a business needs its staff to follow a set of procedures — the flowchart sets out visually what action staff should take.
2) An advantage of flowcharts is that they summarise very complex actions into a set of easy to follow procedures.
3) A disadvantage is that they don't allow for unforeseen events or give staff the flexibility to act on their own initiative.

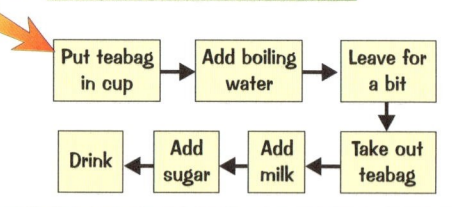

Put teabag in cup → Add boiling water → Leave for a bit → Take out teabag → Add milk → Add sugar → Drink

Brochures, Leaflets and Newsletters are for Customers (mostly)

1) Brochures are like glossy magazines. They are used to help publicise new products or give customers key information about the existing product range.
2) Leaflets are used to inform customers about a new product or an event, such as a sale. They are usually posted to customers or inserted into newspapers or magazines.
3) Businesses tend to use newsletters to keep customers informed of new developments such as new products. They can also be used to inform staff of new policies and general news.
4) Like all written documents, the main advantage of all these is that people can refer back to the document for information. The main disadvantage is that people might lose or ignore it.

My Take That banner is a written communication...

So many things to learn about. It's not too hard though. Reports are just write-ups of investigations, flowcharts are just funny lists with arrows in and the rest are, well, obvious really.

SECTION FOUR — COMMUNICATION

Electronic Communication

Businesses now communicate a lot electronically, mainly through email and the internet. They're not the only methods of electronic communication though. See if you can spot some more...

Paper Documents can be Sent by Fax

Fax machines send and receive copies of paper documents using a telephone line.

The main advantage of fax machines is that documents can be sent quickly for the price of a phone call (i.e. really cheaply).

A disadvantage is that contact can only be made with one fax machine at a time. This means it's time consuming and expensive to send the document to lots of different people.

Another disadvantage is that most boring old fax machines can only print in black and white.

Electronic Messages and Documents can be Sent by Email

Email has replaced fax as the main way we send written messages and documents quickly. Messages can be sent as part of the main email and documents can be attached to the email.

It's easy to send copies of the same email to lots of people at the same time — you just use the carbon copy (Cc) facility. The cost of sending a message is less than a phone call. Plus, the receiver can either print the document themselves or just view it on screen, so unnecessary paperwork isn't created.

The main disadvantage is that both the sender and receiver need access to a computer and the internet. Emails aren't as confidential or as formal as an old-fashioned letter — so wouldn't be appropriate for some types of messages.

The Internet can be Used for Communication

Sometimes businesses want to make information available to the general public, e.g. sales brochures for potential customers. Posting them on a website is a good way of doing this.

An advantage of the internet is that anyone with internet access can view the information. Documents can easily be updated, just by posting the new versions onto the website.

A disadvantage is that the business will not know who has viewed the information. But this can be overcome by asking people to complete a form before downloading the document.

Pagers and Mobile Phones Receive Text Messages

1) Pagers are portable devices that work a bit like mobile phones — except that they only receive messages and can't be used to send messages or make phone calls. They're used by people who need to be contacted in an emergency, for example, doctors on call.

2) As pagers can't send messages, they're being replaced by mobile phones which are more useful.

3) Mobile phones are a useful way for workers to contact each other — especially if they're not working in a fixed location, e.g. sales people.

4) Text messages are used by a few businesses for marketing products to customers. They're useful for short, informal messages. Some customers might find it a bit intrusive though.

Emailing your mates is electronic communication...

Every business worth its salt has a website and the ability to email these days. But this technology only really took off in the 1990s. It's a fast-changing world.

SECTION FOUR — COMMUNICATION

Corporate Image

'Corporation' is another word for an organisation like a business. It's just a fancier term. Corporate image is the opinion that the public has of the business.

Corporate Image Helps a Business to Sell its Products

1) Corporate image is about the reputation of the business. If a business has a strong corporate image, it helps customers to recognise and remember the business — making it more likely that they will choose to buy its products.

2) The presentation of the business's communications is an important part of corporate image, e.g. advertising and publicity, letters and emails, the business's website, and the packaging of products.

3) The type of corporate image a business wants to achieve varies depending on the business's objectives, e.g. a bank might aim for a corporate image of being reliable and customer-oriented, a clothes manufacturer might aim for a corporate image of being luxurious and fashionable.

Corporate Communications Need to Have a Strong Impact

Most businesses try to make sure that all their business communications help reinforce their corporate image. There are a number of rules that businesses follow to achieve this:

1) A logo should be included on all business communications. The logo is a simple, easily recognisable image. It often includes the business's name and an eye-catching design.

2) The business should use the same colour scheme in all of its communications, so that customers will associate that colour scheme with the business.

3) All communications should follow a standard 'house style'. This means that the type of fonts used and the layout of all documents should be the same.

Examples of how corporate image is reinforced in business communications:

1) Letterheads — this is the top part of a letter. Most businesses include the logo in colour alongside the business's name and address.

2) Compliment slips — these are included with any package posted to a stakeholder where a letter is not required. They include the same information as the letterhead, together with space for a short handwritten note.

3) Business cards — these are an important way for salespeople to leave their contact details with a potential customer. They'll include the employee's contact details as well as the business's logo and address.

Public Relations (PR) Helps to Create a Corporate Image

1) Having good business communications is important, but so is having good public relations (PR).

2) Many big businesses have public relations (PR) departments who put out press releases (articles about the company) and organise events that show the firm in a good light.

3) Examples of good PR activities include sponsoring sports teams and supporting charities.

What a vain page — obsessed with image...

Corporate image is important for businesses. For example, whenever you see red and gold you'll probably think of a certain fast food chain... and be reminded that you could go there and eat.

SECTION FOUR — COMMUNICATION

Public Messaging Systems

Public messaging systems give immediate messages or information to staff or customers. There are two main types of public messaging systems — public address systems and bulletin boards.

Public Address Systems are Used for Verbal Messages

1) Public address systems are used in public areas such as shops, schools, airports and railway stations. They use a system of loudspeakers linked to a central microphone.

2) Public address systems are ideal for messages that need to be given to a large group of people — where the people are all in one building but are not all gathered in one particular place.

3) Because the messages are verbal they need to be brief and to the point. Messages should also be repeated as not everyone will hear the message the first time it is given, and some people will not realise that the message is intended for them.

4) Announcers need to be able to speak clearly in a voice that everyone will be able to understand. The message should not be rushed.

5) With older public address systems, it's often difficult to understand the message because the sound comes out of all the speakers at the same time. This means the listener will hear lots of echos when sound reaches them from the other speakers further away. Newer systems try to solve this problem by delaying the message in some speakers to try and minimise the echo.

When you're talking about public address systems, don't make the mistake of calling them 'Tannoys'. Tannoys are just the type of public address system made by Tannoy Ltd. Don't forget.

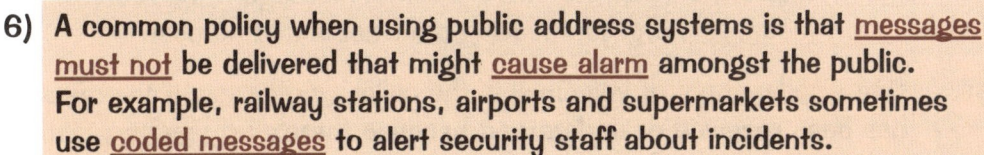

6) A common policy when using public address systems is that messages must not be delivered that might cause alarm amongst the public. For example, railway stations, airports and supermarkets sometimes use coded messages to alert security staff about incidents.

Bulletin Boards are Used for Non-Verbal Information

1) In places such as airports and railway stations the information about departures and arrivals is displayed on bulletin boards. Sometimes they are very large and are designed for hundreds of people to view at the same time. Sometimes they are displayed on small TV-sized monitors.

2) The information is relayed to the monitors electronically and is automatically updated.

3) Bulletin boards are ideal for large amounts of information that is regularly updated.

4) It's important for the information to be checked by staff before being transmitted. This is to ensure that the bulletin board displays correct information using appropriate language and tone.

...there's a lost hotdog in the St John's ambulance area...

If you've ever been to a train station, you'll have seen a bulletin board, and if you've ever been to a country fair you'll understand about the problems public address systems have with echoing...

SECTION FOUR — COMMUNICATION

Verbal Communication

Verbal communication is the most common way in which people communicate in a business. There are four main methods — face to face, telephone, voicemail and video-conferencing.

Face to Face Allows the Receiver to Ask Questions

Face to face conversation happens when two or more people speak to each other at the same time and in the same place (come on, you must have heard of it...). It's good for delivering messages quickly, or for discussing tricky or confidential issues.

The main advantage of it is that you get instant feedback — the person talking can check their message has been understood correctly and the listener can ask questions. People can see each other's body language which helps communication.

The main disadvantage is that no written record of the communication is kept (unless someone takes minutes — see p.38). It can also be unsuitable for very long or complicated messages.

Telephones Allow Long Distance Communication

Telephone conversations are used when people in different locations need to communicate.

The main advantage of telephone communication is that you can speak to somebody who's somewhere else (no shock, Sherlock). It's possible to speak to almost anybody, anywhere in the world. It also allows instant feedback — like a face to face discussion.

The main disadvantage is that it's not possible to see the other person's body language, which can make it harder to interpret the message.

Voicemail Means People Can Leave Verbal Messages

Voicemail is an answer phone system where the caller can leave a verbal message if the receiver is unavailable. It's intended for short messages, e.g. just leaving your name and number.

An advantage of voicemail is that messages can be delivered even when the receiver is unavailable.

One disadvantage of voicemail is the caller won't know if the message has been received or understood because there's no feedback with the recipient. Another disadvantage is that most voicemail systems have a limit to the length of a message, so messages can get cut off.

Video-Conferencing Saves Travelling to Meetings

Video-conferencing works in the same way as telephone conference calls, except that a visual image is also transmitted. It's suitable when a lengthy discussion is required between people located in different parts of the world.

The main advantage is that it lets a group of people in different places share ideas. Also participants can see each other's body language.

A disadvantage is that all participants need access to video-conferencing technology. It can also be difficult to view all the participants at the same time and it's more expensive than a telephone conference.

Chatting to your mates is verbal communication...

Video-conferencing probably takes quite some getting used to. It's hard enough talking to a group of people who all want to talk at once... But imagine all their faces being on a monitor. Weird.

SECTION FOUR — COMMUNICATION

Meetings

Meetings are a big part of business life. They are often used to discuss issues and make decisions. They can be formal or informal, depending on the circumstances.

Informal Meetings can Happen Off the Cuff

1) Any work-related discussion between two or more people classes as an informal meeting.
2) Informal meetings happen when there is something that needs to be discussed urgently, or when there's an issue that needs to be discussed which isn't important enough for a formal meeting.

> Informal meetings can be useful because they allow issues to be discussed at short notice. Plus, there's no need to prepare the documents needed for a formal meeting (see below).

> Because there's no formal record of what was discussed or agreed at an informal meeting, it can be difficult to monitor progress following the meeting. Another problem with informal meetings is that some relevant issues might not get discussed if there's limited time to prepare for the meeting or if there isn't an agenda to remind people.

Formal Meetings Need More Planning

1) A formal meeting is planned and organised in advance. Formal meetings are usually held so that people can discuss specific issues. Some formal meetings take place at regular intervals, for example, a monthly meeting of all sales staff.
2) Formal meetings have a notice of meeting and an agenda which are sent to participants before the meeting. They also have minutes which are circulated after the meeting (see p.38).
3) All formal meetings need a chairperson — they decide who will speak at the meeting and when it's time to move on to the next item on the agenda.

> An advantage of formal, planned meetings is that the participants have time to prepare for the issues being discussed. A formal written record (minutes) of the meeting is kept, so participants know what has been discussed and agreed.

> A disadvantage is that often there's a limit to the issues that can be included on the agenda. Also it takes time to organise a formal meeting — informal meetings are better for responding quickly to events.

Lots of Factors Contribute to a Well-Organised Meeting

For a formal meeting to run smoothly, there are lots of things for the organiser to think about:

1) The notice of meeting, the agenda and any other necessary documents need to be prepared and sent out before the meeting. The minutes also need to be given out afterwards.
2) Sometimes the participants at the meeting have not met before. Ice-breaker activities can help get people talking at the start so they feel more comfortable talking during the meeting. These activities need to be planned before the meeting.
3) The meeting room will need to be booked in advance. Any special equipment needed, such as projectors, will have to be arranged. If some participants are travelling to the meeting, transport and accommodation may need to be organised.

A good meeting needs doughnuts...
You could argue that a reason for meetings is for bored, lonely office workers to meet up, have a chat, drink tea and generally avoid doing any work. But then you wouldn't get any marks for that.

SECTION FOUR — COMMUNICATION

Choosing a Communication Channel

This is a popular topic for examiners. Make sure you know how to decide which is the most appropriate method to communicate a particular message.

There are Five Criteria for Choosing a Communication Method

① THE NATURE OF THE MESSAGE TO BE DELIVERED

1) If a message is confidential or sensitive then how it's delivered should reflect this. Sometimes it's important that no one but the intended recipient should receive the message.

2) Lengthy or complicated messages should be written down to make sure all the points are clearly explained and the receiver can read through the information again.

3) Messages that are part of a legal process should always be written and sent by post. E.g. part of a complicated business transaction such as buying and selling property.

② THE NUMBER OF RECIPIENTS

A message that needs to be sent to lots of people in different places should ideally be a written message that can be read by all the intended recipients — it could be by letter, email or newsletter. Alternatively, if only one person needs to be given the message a meeting might be a better method to use.

③ THE URGENCY OF THE MESSAGE

Messages that can wait a couple of days can be posted in a letter or put on a noticeboard. Urgent messages can be emailed or faxed. If it's important to confirm that the message has been received then a phone call might be the best method.

④ THE COST OF SENDING THE MESSAGE

1) Two of the most expensive ways to deliver a message are by telephoning somebody living abroad or travelling to deliver a face to face message. The cheapest method of communicating with them is probably to email them.

2) But sometimes the cheapest method is not the most appropriate. For example, it is better to hold a discussion face to face or over the telephone, instead of by email.

⑤ THE LANGUAGES SPOKEN BY THE RECIPIENT

1) Some people are better at reading a foreign language than speaking it. These people would prefer to communicate in the foreign language through written rather than verbal methods.

2) Time zones also matter when communicating abroad. When it is 9am in London it is 4am in New York. So if the message can wait it is better to phone them after 1pm in London. Otherwise an email message might be better.

Example of a message and the appropriate communication method

A personnel manager wants to invite six people for a job interview. She needs to give each applicant details of when and where the interviews will be held. If the interviews are more than two weeks away, then a letter would be the most appropriate method. If they are less than two weeks away then it might be better to phone the applicants first and then offer to email or fax the details.

Carrier pigeon or email? — hmm, that's a tricky one...

It's important stuff, this. I can imagine an exam question on it... The best way to learn it is probably by reading it over a couple of times and then trying to write it out as a mini-essay. Fun.

SECTION FOUR — COMMUNICATION

Communication Procedures and Policies

Businesses have policies and procedures to help staff use communications effectively.

Businesses have Procedures for Handling Communications

1) A common policy is for junior staff to have their outgoing written communication checked by a supervisor or manager before it is sent. This is to ensure the tone and content of the message reflect the business's image.

2) Another common policy is that all incoming mail is seen by a department manager before being given to the appropriate member of staff. This makes sure each member of staff only gets communications relevant to their job and that messages are dealt with effectively.

3) Business often have different procedures for internal and external communications. For example, supervisors might not check written communication if it is only being sent internally.

4) Sometimes there are policies about verbal communications, e.g. how phone calls are dealt with.

> For example a common phone policy might state that:
> 1) All telephone calls should be answered quickly — e.g. within four rings.
> 2) All staff should say the company name and their name at the start of the call.
> 3) Staff should try to solve the query in a positive, helpful way.
> 4) Staff who are absent from their desk should divert their calls to another phone or switch on their voicemail.

Communication Policies Vary Depending on the Business Type

1) Communication procedures can vary depending on the size of the business. A small business may have quite informal communication procedures. A large business which needs to train large numbers of staff (e.g. a supermarket chain) is more likely to have fixed procedures.

2) The culture of the business and its leadership style affects how communications are dealt with, e.g. a company with a strong, authoritarian leadership style is more likely to monitor employee communications than one with a more relaxed leadership style.

3) Businesses need to ensure customers have a positive experience when dealing with staff. Workplaces where staff deal regularly with customers (e.g. call centres and shops) are likely to have detailed procedures about communication.

Communication Equipment Needs to be Used Effectively

Procedures can ensure that communication is used effectively, e.g.

1) Fax messages should be sent with a cover sheet explaining who the message has been sent from and who the intended recipient is.

2) Senior Managers and Directors often have their Personal Assistant (PA) filter their calls to make sure that they only deal with issues that cannot be dealt with by junior staff.

3) Direct telephone lines are often installed for sales and customer support staff. This enables customers to directly contact the staff without having to go through the company switchboard.

Communication Policy No.44 — be silent as a monk...

Phew. At last — you've finished the section. Now you should be an expert on communication. Bet you still find it hard to write thank you letters and the like though, despite your new skills.

Revision Summary for Section Four

Ooh look — some lovely questions. Just what you wanted to celebrate finishing the section...

1) Define communication.
2) List four reasons why businesses need to communicate internally.
3) Why do businesses need to have good external communications?
4) What are the three main methods of communication?
5) Why is a long chain of command bad for communications?
6) Name the three types of communication network.
7) How can good internal communication help a business?
8) List the four main barriers to communication.
9) Why might a business choose to send a business letter?
    a) Because a formal record of the message needs to be kept.
    b) Because someone ordered too much paper and it needs to be used up.
    c) To invite a member of staff to a meeting.
10) Give two disadvantages of sending business letters.
11) List the seven standard items that appear on an agenda.
12) What document is the formal record of a meeting?
13) What is 'memo' short for?
14) Give one advantage of using memos.
15) List three disadvantages of using notices.
16) Why are reports written?
17) List the six main sections that should be included in a report.
18) What do flowcharts summarise?
19) Give an advantage of documents like brochures and leaflets.
20) Give one disadvantage for businesses of using fax machines.
21) What's replaced fax as the main technology for sending written messages and documents quickly?
22) Why would a business give its staff pagers?
23) Where are public address systems usually used?
24) What is a disadvantage of face to face communication?
25) List two advantages of telephone communication.
26) Give two advantages of informal meetings.
27) What is a disadvantage of formal meetings?
28) List the five criteria that should be considered when choosing a communication method.
29) Give three reasons why businesses have procedures and policies for handling communications.

SECTION FOUR — COMMUNICATION

Computers and Networks

You need to know about the different types of computer and how they're connected together.

PCs are the Most Common Computers

1) PCs (Personal Computers) were designed to stand alone, but are now often linked together in a network.
2) PCs can be either desktops or laptops (also called notebooks).
3) Desktops often have more facilities than laptops. Laptops can be used anywhere because they can run on battery power, but they use an LCD monitor which can easily be damaged. Laptops are also more expensive, and can be lost.

Who are you calling common, sunshine?

> Palmtops or Personal Digital Assistants (PDAs) were originally used instead of a diary. They now contain many of the same applications as desktops and laptops, such as spreadsheets and word processors.

A Network is Two or More Computers Connected Together

See Big Brother last night?
Ooh I can't stand that Chantelle...

1) Computers can be connected to a network so they can communicate with each other.
2) A computer needs a network interface card to connect to a network.

A LAN is a Small, Local Network

LANs (Local Area Networks) are the networks that you find in most offices. They usually need the following hardware in order to operate:

- A Network File Server is a dedicated computer that runs the software needed by the network and stores the files that users have created.
- Terminals are individual workstations that give access to the network's software and files.
- If a group of terminals shares use of a printer, then the system needs a print server. If more than one document is sent to the printer, the print server will put them into a queue.
- For the network to operate, data needs to be sent to and from all parts of the network. This can be done using wire cables or fibre optic cables, or via radio signals.

NOTE — a LAN doesn't have to include a server. LANs can be as simple as two or three computers linked together for sharing files or software.

Com-put-er, you say? Nope, never heard of one of those...

Doubtless you already knew a thing or two about what this thing called a 'computer' is before you read this page. But don't relax — this is just to ease you in. Things get trickier from now on...

Computers and Networks

This page has information on some more types of networks.

WANs are Long Range Networks

1) WAN is short for Wide Area Network. WANs are used when the computers that need to be connected together are in different places.

2) WANs need servers to operate the network, but users connect to the network using modems, usually connected to the telephone system. Wireless technology such as microwaves or satellite can also be used — but this can be expensive.

3) WANs are used by companies who have employees working away from the firm's main sites. A good example would be oil exploration engineers who work in remote parts of the world.

The Internet is an International Network of Computers

1) The Internet is basically a very big WAN.

2) The Internet was originally developed by the US Government to improve communication between its military computers. But it's since grown into what we all know today.

3) Today many companies, even small ones, have their own websites on the internet. Any documents intended for people outside the organisation, such as brochures, can be put on the website for them to download.

An Intranet is a Company's Private Network

1) Using an intranet, documents can be produced in electronic form and made available to other staff within the company.

2) An intranet can be a LAN or a WAN, depending on the size of the company.

Advantages of using networks

1) Peripherals such as printers can be shared among many different users.
2) Terminals are cheaper than stand-alone PCs.
3) Software can be shared among users.
4) Communication is cheap and fast.

Disadvantages of using networks

1) Cabling can be expensive to install and replace.
2) A fault with the server will prevent the whole network from working.
3) Security measures are needed to restrict access to the network.
4) WANS are vulnerable to hackers and viruses.

Networks — I don' WAN' do this...

Don't get LANs and WANs confused — they're easy to remember if you just learn what the L and the W stand for. One reason companies use an intranet is to try to create a paperless office, where cumbersome printed documents are a thing of the past. Keep on dreaming...

SECTION FIVE — ICT IN THE BUSINESS ENVIRONMENT

Networks — Different Configurations

Network configurations are also known as network topologies. Some of this stuff is a wee bit tricky. But if you give it a bit of thought, the pros and cons of each type are pretty obvious. If you're studying the AQA syllabus you don't need to learn the stuff on this page.

Star Networks Give Access to a Central Computer

1) Star networks are used when a large number of workstations need to be connected to a central computer.
2) Each workstation is connected directly to the central computer.

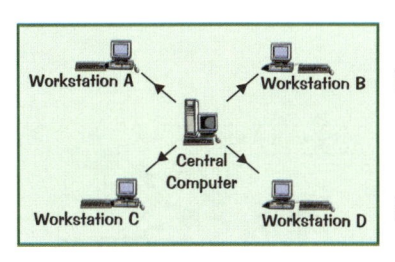

PROS
1) Performance in one part of the network is unaffected by events elsewhere.
2) Cable failure is less of a problem.

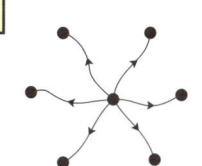

CONS
1) Failure in the central computer causes the whole network to break down.
2) Uses more cabling, so it's more expensive.

Bus Networks are the Cheapest

1) In bus networks (line networks) data is sent to and from the file server along a line of cable.
2) All terminals are connected to this central line.

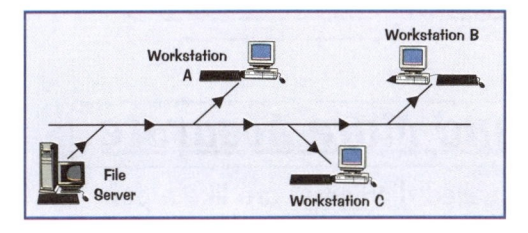

PROS
1) Cheap — because it uses less cabling.
2) Easy to install.

CONS
1) With lots of users the system becomes very slow, as all data goes along a central line.
2) Failure of the central cable will bring the whole network down.

Ring Networks are Faster than Bus Networks

1) Ring networks are a bit like bus networks, except that all the equipment is linked in a ring.
2) Data flows around the network in one direction only.

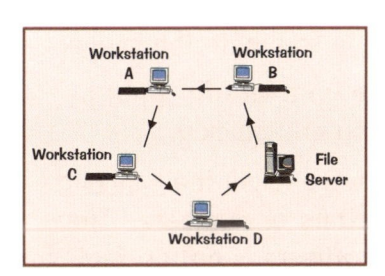

PROS
1) Cheap to expand.
2) Fast — as data flows in one direction only.

CONS
1) With lots of users the system can slow down, as all the data is sent along a single line.
2) Failure of the central cable brings the whole network down.

The definition of lazy — when your network is zero...

There's some tricky stuff on this page. But all you need to know is the three most common network topologies, and what their advantages and disadvantages are. Try writing a song about it, or a poem or something. Or even more fun — yes I know — jot down a wee mini-essay on it.

SECTION FIVE — ICT IN THE BUSINESS ENVIRONMENT

Input Devices

An input device is any hardware which is used to enter data into the computer system.

QWERTY Keyboards are the Most Common Input Device

1) QWERTY keyboards are based on the way typewriters were designed. The name comes from the first row of letters on the keyboard.
2) A problem is that keying in can be slow unless the user has been trained to type.
3) They are also related to injuries such as repetitive strain injury (RSI).

A Mouse is a Type of Pointing Device

1) The movement of the ball underneath the mouse is related to the movement of the cursor on the screen. An optical mouse uses a light sensor instead of a ball.
2) Frequently using a mouse can cause repetitive strain injury.

He went thadda way.

Instead of a mouse, laptops have different pointing devices:
- A tracker-ball works in the same way as a mouse, but the ball's moved by hand. It takes up less space than a mouse, but they are slow and not very accurate.
- With touch-sensitive pads, you move your finger across the pad to move the cursor. They use less space than a mouse, but they're easily damaged and not very reliable.

Graphics Pads make Drawing Easier and More Accurate

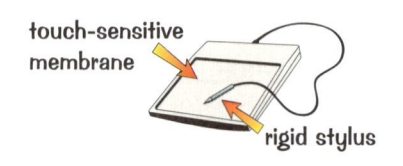

touch-sensitive membrane
rigid stylus

1) Graphics tablets (sometimes called digitisers) are like a pen and paper. They're made of a touch-sensitive membrane (like the piece of paper) and a rigid stylus (like the pen).
2) Many people find graphics pads are easier to use and more accurate than mice, although they are fairly expensive.

Scanners Convert Images into Digital Data

1) A picture is passed through the scanner and is converted into digital data to create the image.
2) A problem is that the bitmap files created can be very large and so take up a lot of memory. A benefit is that the scanned image can be manipulated and edited easily and quickly.
3) OCR (Optical Character Recognition) scanners can read text. The software takes the scanned digital information and looks for familiar patterns that might make up letters or numbers. The scanned text can be edited using word-processing software. But the software is not perfect so mistakes can occur, and most OCR software cannot cope with text in columns.

Learn about the mouse? — what a drag...

It's really important you know what the pros and cons of the different input devices are. You might think this kind of gadgetry's nothing new, but you have to know when it's useful and when it's not.

Input Devices

Can't get enough of input devices? Well here's some more for you.

MICR is used for Cheques and OMR is used for Registers

MICR — Magnetic Ink Character Recognition

MICR is used by banks to process the payment of cheques. At the bottom of cheques are numbers printed with ink containing iron. When the ink is magnetised a scanner can read the numbers and so know which account to take the money from. This is very fast and almost 100% accurate. But the system is very expensive.

OMR — Optical Mark Recognition

OMR is used in some schools to take the daily class register. The teacher fills in different boxes with a pencil if a pupil is present or absent. A scanner detects the carbon in the boxes on the page and inputs the data into the computer system. The system is quick and accurate — but only if the OMR sheet is filled in properly.

Magnetic Stripes are used on Credit Cards

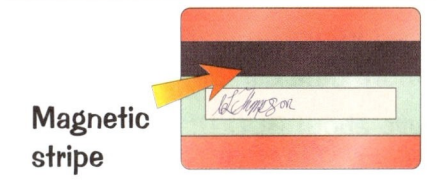

Magnetic stripe

1) Magnetic stripe cards use a short length of magnetic tape sealed into the surface on the back of a plastic card.
2) They carry information so the computer can identify the customer (credit/debit cards) or the number of units available (phone cards).
3) Most cards now have a chip which carries the information — the customer also has a PIN to confirm their identity.

Digital Cameras and Webcams Save Images as Pixels

Digital cameras save an image as a series of dots called pixels. The image can be uploaded to a computer and edited. A webcam works in a similar way but can send real-time images over the net.

BENEFIT — Photographic film is not needed and the image is available for immediate use. It can also be sent via an e-mail attachment to anywhere in the world.

PROBLEM — High-resolution images use lots of memory and battery power.

Light Pens or Laser Scanners read Bar Codes

Light pens and laser scanners are used in places like supermarkets and libraries to read a bar code which contains data about the product being scanned.

BENEFIT — It makes buying goods faster and reduces the chance of human error.

PROBLEM — The system is expensive and depends on the accuracy of the data stored.

Microphones are an Increasingly Common Input Device

Microphones are used to input data into voice-recognition systems, which convert sound into text or commands for the computer. They can also record sound so it can be stored digitally and sent over the Internet or by email.

BENEFIT — You can use dictation instead of having to type.

PROBLEM — The data uses a lot of memory.

"Show me the way to Amarillo..."

Please sir, tell me more about reading bar codes...

There you are, two whole pages on input devices. And they just get more exciting as you go on. From the dull old keyboard to the unadulterated fun of the microphone.

SECTION FIVE — ICT IN THE BUSINESS ENVIRONMENT

Data Storage

Businesses have a huge amount of data that needs to be stored securely and accessed easily. There are now a number of storage devices available to them.

There are Internal and External Storage Devices

1) There are two main types of computer storage facilities — internal devices (which are part of the computer hardware) and external devices (which are separate from the individual computer).

2) Most companies use internal devices as the main form of storage. External devices are used mainly for data back up and to transfer saved data files between different computers.

The Hard Disk is the Main Internal Storage Device

Whadda you lookin at?

1) The size of the hard disk is measured in gigabytes (Gb) — the more gigabytes there are the more data can be stored.

2) Today most desktop computers have about 300 Gb of storage space on their hard drive and most laptops have 40 to 120 Gb.

3) The desktop storage space is enough to store most of the data needed for a small to medium sized company. It depends on the type of data that is kept though — multimedia data takes up more space.

4) If the hard drive fails all data can be lost. This causes serious difficulties for the business such as losing customer addresses. For this reason, back-ups of data files on the hard disk must always be kept on an external storage device.

5) Also, hard disks aren't easily portable. To access data from another machine, users need to copy data on to an external storage device or connect to a LAN or WAN within the company.

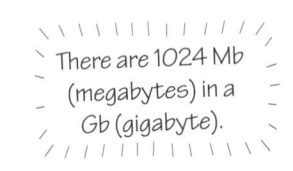

There are 1024 Mb (megabytes) in a Gb (gigabyte).

Floppy Disks are an External Storage Device

Floppy disks (3.5 inch disks) used to be the most common external storage device.

Advantages of floppy disks
- They are small, portable and cheap.
- Data can be transferred quickly between different computers.

Disadvantages of floppy disks
- They can only store about 1.44 Mb of data. A huge number of disks would be needed to store all the data produced by even a small business.
- They are easily corrupted, resulting in lost data.

Back-up punk, or I just might lose my temper...

The important thing about data is that whatever happens, data must not be lost and needs to be available to the business when required. Businesses have to decide how to ensure this happens.

SECTION FIVE — ICT IN THE BUSINESS ENVIRONMENT

Data Storage

Modern external storage devices can hold a lot more data than floppy disks.

Optical Devices use Lasers to Store Data

Compact Discs (CDs)

CDs hold about 650 Mb of data. There are several different types:

1) **CD-ROMs** are read only — the data held on them can't be altered. They're used to distribute computer software such as Microsoft® Office.

2) **CD-R** works by using a special drive to write data to a blank CD. It can only be written once. The main problem is that you can't edit the file once it has been written to the CD. If you want to change the file, you have to save it again separately, using up more disk space.

3) **CD-RW (Rewrite)** also needs a special drive but has the advantage that the disk can be wiped and reused. It's possible to save textual, video and audio data on CDs but they are limited by size. The quality of video material is not as good as on the newer types of data storage.

Digital Versatile Discs (DVDs)

DVDs are like CDs but hold more data — up to 17 Gb. They provide much better quality video playback but each blank DVD disk is more expensive.

Memory Sticks

I'd never remember my recipe for toadstool broth without it.

1) Memory sticks can hold up to 5 Gb of data. They are small enough to be carried in a pocket or purse.

2) Frequent saving to the memory stick causes it to burn out so the data on the stick should be backed up elsewhere.

3) There can also be problems of security. Some businesses don't allow their employees to use memory sticks because it would be too easy to copy confidential information or transfer viruses onto company networks.

Non-Optical Devices can also be used to Back Up Data

1) ZIP drives store data on disks similar to floppy disks, but are bigger and hold up to 250 Mb of data. The development of DVD-RW disks is now making ZIP drives obsolete.

2) Magnetic Tape is used by most companies using networks and hard drives to back up their data. It's cheap and can store all the company computerised data. Most companies will send their tapes offsite so that data can be recovered in case of a disaster.

3) It's also possible to access internet files of text and music by saving links to internet sites. This allows them to be accessed quickly and does not take up storage space on users' machines.

4) A disadvantage is the website could be removed by the person or organisation that originated it.

Don't leave your ZIP drive undone...

Magnetic tape sounds like it could be really fun doesn't it? Using it to play tricks on people while they're listening to their walkman or something... but alas no. It's used to back data up. Great.

SECTION FIVE — ICT IN THE BUSINESS ENVIRONMENT

Output Devices — Printers

An <u>output device</u> is any hardware used to communicate the result of data processing. For example, <u>printers</u> are used to produce a permanent hard copy of the information.

Dot-Matrix Printers are Old-Fashioned and Slow

Dot-matrix printers are also called <u>impact printers</u>. They have two main parts:

1) The <u>printhead</u> is a <u>matrix of pins</u> — either 9 or 24 pins. Each <u>character</u> is formed by using a <u>set pattern</u> of pins.

2) The <u>ribbon</u> is a long strip of material with ink on one side. The printhead pins <u>push</u> the ribbon onto the printer paper to print a series of <u>dots</u>, which form the <u>characters</u>.

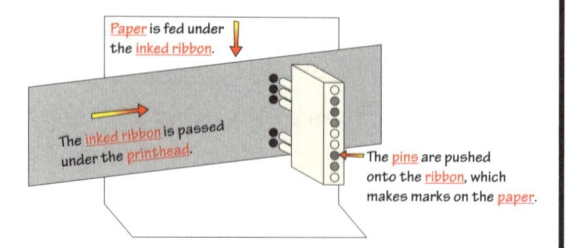

Advantages of Dot-Matrix Printers
1) Quite <u>cheap</u> to buy and have low operating costs.
2) Can print on <u>continuous stationery</u> or <u>multi-part stationery</u> (e.g. copies of invoices).

Disadvantages of Dot-Matrix Printers
1) <u>Low resolution</u> — print quality is too poor to produce presentation documents.
2) <u>Very slow</u> — can be less than 100 characters per minute (cpm).
3) <u>Very noisy</u> — can't be used near a phone.

Laser Printers are Popular and Good Quality

Laser printers are called <u>page printers</u> because the data to be printed is sent to the printer in complete pages — one page at a time. They have <u>four main parts</u>:

1) <u>Electrostatic rotating drum</u> — has an electrical charge.
2) <u>Laser</u> — etches onto the drum a <u>negative image</u> of the page to be printed. Where the laser hits the drum the electrical charge is <u>removed</u>.
3) <u>Toner cartridge</u> — contains <u>ink</u>. When the drum passes over the toner cartridge the ink is <u>attracted</u> onto the charged areas of the drum. The ink is then <u>transferred</u> onto the printer paper.
4) <u>Fuser unit</u> — heats the paper to <u>fuse the ink</u> onto it.

Advantages of Laser Printers
1) <u>High resolution</u> — typically 600 dots per inch (dpi) or more. This means they can print high-quality documents.
2) <u>Fast</u> — over 10 pages per minute (ppm).
3) Laser printers are <u>very quiet</u>.

Disadvantages of Laser Printers
1) <u>Quite expensive</u> — though they're getting cheaper.
2) Lots of <u>complex equipment</u> inside — so <u>expensive to repair</u>.
3) <u>Can't</u> use continuous or multi-part stationery.

The Dot-Matrix — featuring June Brown and Keanu Reeves...

Dot-matrix printers are a bit old hat these days. Laser printers are much better — they're good quality, fast and don't make an annoying chugging noise...

SECTION FIVE — ICT IN THE BUSINESS ENVIRONMENT

Output Devices — Printers

Knowing about the different types of printers is really important — that's why they get two pages.

Ink-Jet Printers are Cheap and Reasonable Quality

1) These cost less than laser printers and produce better quality printouts than dot-matrix printers.

2) The main component is the printhead. This has lots of tiny nozzles or spouts through which small jets of ink are sprayed onto the paper.

3) There are three different ways of controlling the flow of ink. In some inkjet printers, the nozzles are controlled by crystals inside the printhead. In others, the ink is heated so that it expands and pushes through the nozzles onto the paper. Continuous flow printers squirt ink continuously from the nozzles.

4) There are loads more nozzles on an ink-jet than dots on a dot-matrix — so the print resolution (quality) is better.

5) A bubble-jet printer is an ink-jet printer that works by heating the ink.

Advantages of Ink-Jet Printers
1) Good resolution — usually 300 to 600 dots per inch (dpi). This means they can print good quality documents (and often in colour).
2) Cheap to buy.
3) Small — so ideal for home or office desk use.

Disadvantages of Ink-Jet Printers
1) Slow(ish) — colour printing often less than 4 pages per minute.
2) Quite expensive to run — the cartridges cost more (per page) than laser printer cartridges.

Choose your Printer Wisely

Because of the differences between the printers, they're all suited to different situations.

Use a DOT-MATRIX if you want to print lots of copies of the same text but aren't worried about noise, quality or speed.

Use an INK-JET if you want good quality affordable printing — but not a lot of it.

Use a LASER if you want to print loads of pages of professional quality documents quickly.

I was going to use a laser to take over the world. But now I work in publishing...

Graph Plotters are Specialised Printers

1) Laser printers are good for most things but they're often not accurate enough for precision drawings such as architects' plans — and they can't print on big enough bits of paper.

2) The most common graph plotter is a flat-bed plotter. The paper lies on a flat surface and a plotter arm moves over it from left to right. On the plotter arm is a pen holder which moves up and down. In this way the pen can draw accurate images in any direction.

3) As colour laser printers get cheaper and better there will be less demand for small graph plotters.

A printer settled the argument — it had good resolution...

Yup, printers have certainly come a long way in recent times, and there sure are plenty to choose from. Ink-jets are usually the best compromise between quality and affordability.

SECTION FIVE — ICT IN THE BUSINESS ENVIRONMENT

Other Kinds of Output Device

Think you're finished with output devices? Think again. There's more to them than just printers you know.

VDU is a posh word for a Monitor

1) The VDUs (Visual Display Units) used by businesses depend on the type of work being carried out. E.g. Design work needs large, clear screens.

2) More straightforward work like word processing or entering data into a database can be done on cheaper, smaller screens with a lower resolution (less clear picture).

3) VDUs are changing — laptops and desktop computers are now usually supplied with LCD flat screens. These take up less space on desks and produce a clearer visual image. However, they are easier to damage and are often more expensive.

Microfilm can be used to Store Lots of Information

1) Businesses have to keep all sorts of records such as personnel files and financial information stored for years.

2) They can save on the amount of paper needed by taking photographs of the original pages and storing them on microfilm. This can later be magnified and reprinted if needed. These photographed documents can be viewed on computers or microfilm readers.

Advantages of Microfilm
1) Reduces the storage space required.
2) Film lasts much longer than paper.

Disadvantages of Microfilm
1) The system is expensive.
2) Losing one roll of microfilm will lose loads of information.

LCD Projectors make presentations much easier

1) LCD projectors are another type of output device. They can be connected to a laptop or desktop computer.

2) Whatever appears on the computer monitor is projected onto a screen so that it can be viewed by an audience.

3) They're used for training, sales presentations and business meetings.

Advantages of LCD Projectors
1) No need to load awkward slides.
2) Video images can be displayed.
3) Light and portable.

Disadvantages of LCD Projectors
1) More expensive than an overhead projector.
2) Require the user to have a computer.
3) Sometimes hard to use without a remote control.

Microfilms — anything starring Danny DeVito...

The development of the LCD projector means that the days of training sessions descending into chaos as dull corporate slides appear upside down will soon be a thing of the past. More's the pity.

SECTION FIVE — ICT IN THE BUSINESS ENVIRONMENT

ICT Systems

When choosing an ICT system businesses need to consider a number of factors.

The System Should Match the Business's Needs

1) **EASE OF USE** — Complicated ICT systems are expensive as the company may have to employ specialist staff or retrain current staff to use and maintain the system.
2) **FITNESS FOR THE PURPOSE NEEDED** — The company should buy hardware and software that will meet its current needs and be capable of expansion as the business grows.
3) **COST OF EQUIPMENT** — Buying hardware that's too powerful will be a waste of money. Companies must also take into account how much it will cost to run equipment such as printers and copiers. They also need to assess maintenance and support costs.

Rubbish, I've never poked a system in my life.

Bespoke systems are designed especially for the company, so they can be tailored for the exact purpose required. But they're more expensive than "off the shelf" applications such as Microsoft® Office and staff may need extra training to use them.

Environmental Factors are also Important

Disposal of hardware

1) Computer hardware must now be disposed of by specialist companies.
2) These companies make sure that all data is removed from hard disks and disassemble machines so that components are disposed of safely.

Power saving

1) Modern computers, which often have to be on for 24 hours a day, are equipped with power saving facilities.
2) This makes sure that the business does not have to pay for more power than needed when machines are not in use.
3) It also saves electricity, helping to reduce the quantity of carbon emissions produced.

Health and safety

1) The equipment a company buys must meet health and safety requirements.
2) Input devices such as keyboards should be designed to reduce the risk of causing repetitive strain injury (RSI) to users.
3) Furniture should be adjustable to ensure good posture. Screens should not give out high levels of radiation or cause eye strain to users.
4) Cables need to be positioned so that they cannot be tripped over. They could be sunk into the floor or into channels attached to the wall.

Bespoke systems — specially designed for bicycle wheels...

Companies are legally required to consider environmental issues. So if you see your boss sneaking off to the landfill site with a big bag that makes clunking noises, it's time to call Johnny Law.

SECTION FIVE — ICT IN THE BUSINESS ENVIRONMENT

Revision Summary for Section Five

You're nearly at the end of the section, so take a well-earned break. Did you enjoy it? Right, now answer all these questions about ICT in Business. What? You don't want to? Do you want me to come round to your house with a megaphone and recite the whole chapter to you while you're trying to sleep? Thought not. So have a go — you might know more than you think.

1) What advantages do laptops have over desktop PCs?
2) Name two problems associated with laptops.
3) What does PDA stand for?
4) What does a computer need in order to be able to connect to a network?
5) What kind of network is usually found in offices?
6) Give one reason why a company would use a WAN.
7) Give three advantages and three disadvantages of using a network.
8) For each of the following network configurations, give an advantage and a disadvantage:
   a) star networks,
   b) bus networks,
   c) ring networks.
9) What is meant by 'input device'?
10) What type of injury can be caused by both keyboards and mice?
11) Why might a graphics pad be a better choice than a mouse when using graphics programs?
12) How can an OCR scanner be useful?
13) Name two input devices that can be used to read bar codes.
14) Why should a company always back up data saved on a hard drive?
15) Name two problems with floppy disks.
16) What advantages do DVDs have over CDs?
17) Give an advantage and a disadvantage of memory sticks.
18) What does "output device" mean?
19) Name two advantages and two disadvantages each for:
   a) dot-matrix printers,
   b) laser printers,
   c) inkjet printers.
20) How does a graph plotter work?
21) What does VDU stand for?
22) What might a company use microfilm for?
23) Why is it risky to use microfilm?
24) How can an LCD projector make presentations easier? What are the drawbacks?
25) Give one benefit and one drawback of using bespoke ICT systems.
26) Describe three ways of making sure ICT systems meet health and safety standards.

SECTION SIX — MONEY TRANSFERS & E-COMMERCE

Payment Systems

The next two pages cover the different ways payments can be made. ICT systems have had a big impact on payment systems and the speed payments are made. If you're studying the AQA syllabus you can skip straight to page 63 on telephone and internet banking.

Cash is the Simplest Payment Method

1) Cash is notes and coins. To make a cash payment you simply hand over the cash to the payee.

2) Cash is quicker than paying by cheque and the payee can spend the money straight away. But it is an insecure payment method — cash is easy to steal or lose. Also, no record is kept of the money transfer, unless the business records it manually.

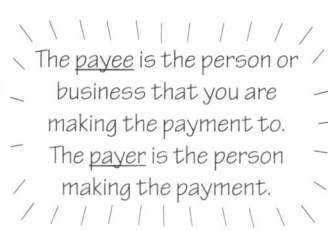

The payee is the person or business that you are making the payment to. The payer is the person making the payment.

Cheques are a Written Instruction to Transfer Money

The payer writes a cheque and gives it to the payee. The payee gives the cheque to their bank who process the cheque. The payee's bank requests the money from the payer's bank account and the bank will transfer money electronically.

1) An advantage of cheques is that they are more secure than using cash. Also a record is kept of the payment.

2) A disadvantage is that it can take three days before a cheque is processed and paid. It can take even longer to process if the cheque details contain errors — e.g. if it is unsigned.

3) Signatures can be forged — leading to cheque fraud.

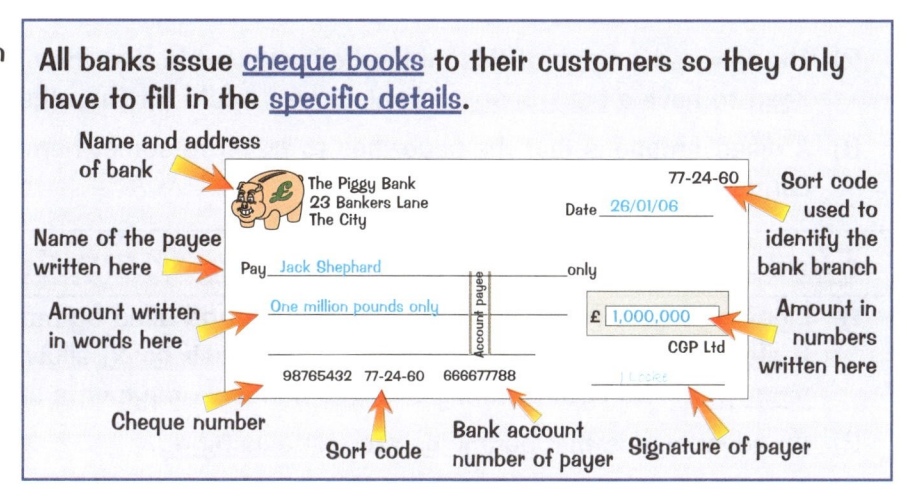

All banks issue cheque books to their customers so they only have to fill in the specific details.

- Name and address of bank: The Piggy Bank, 23 Bankers Lane, The City
- Sort code used to identify the bank branch: 77-24-60
- Date: 26/01/06
- Name of the payee written here: Pay Jack Shephard
- Amount written in words here: One million pounds only
- Amount in numbers written here: £1,000,000
- CGP Ltd
- Cheque number: 98765432
- Sort code: 77-24-60
- Bank account number of payer: 666677788
- Signature of payer

The Payee Requests the Payment for a Direct Debit

1) A direct debit is an instruction for payment from the payee's bank to the payer's bank. Money will only be paid if the payer has agreed to let their bank make a payment to the payee.

2) Direct debits are often used to pay bills. For example, the electricity company might send a bill every three months which says how much the payment will be and when it will be collected. The payer does not need to do anything — the bill will be paid by the payer's bank.

3) The main advantage is that the payment is automatic — the payee usually has a computer that generates the payment request automatically (see EDI on page 62).

4) A disadvantage is that the payer has to make sure there is enough money in the account to pay the bill.

The supermarket wouldn't accept my chocolate coins...

They wouldn't accept my monopoly money either, or the piece of chewing gum and three paper clips I had in my pocket — all I wanted was a newspaper and some sandwiches.

Payment Systems

Look — even more payment systems. I bet you can't wait to get started on these. (Not for AQA.)

Standing Orders are for a Regular Fixed Amount

1) Standing orders are similar to direct debits. They are often used to pay for goods bought on a credit agreement. The buyer agrees to pay a fixed amount to the payee's account for a fixed period and the buyer's bank transfers the money. At the end of the agreed period the standing order stops.

2) An advantage is that it is a secure, electronic payment. Also the buyer does not need to do anything once the standing order is set up because the payment is automatic.

3) A disadvantage is that the buyer needs to ensure they have enough money in their account each month to cover the payment.

Credit Transfer — the Payer Doesn't Need a Bank Account

1) Some businesses, such as electricity suppliers, allow their customers to pay by credit transfer. The bill they send to the customer contains a payment slip at the bottom. The customer uses the slip to pay the bill at a bank or post office. The payment can be a cheque or cash. The bank or post office then arranges for the cheque or cash to be transferred to the business's bank account.

2) The main advantage of this method of payment is that the payer does not need to have a bank account (which they would for the other systems).

3) A disadvantage is that the payer has to travel to somewhere they can pay the bill.

Can I pay my bill with these magic beans? I've got my payment slip.

Electronic Data Interchange Uses Computers to Make Payments

1) Electronic Data Interchange (EDI) is the method used by most businesses to transfer money. It electronically links businesses directly to their bank, allowing them to make immediate payments. No actual money changes hands — payments are made using BACS (see below).

2) An advantage is that payments are made instantly.

3) A disadvantage is that employees still need to instruct a computer to make or request a payment, so there is a risk of human error.

BACS is Becoming Increasingly Common

1) Banks Automated Clearing System (BACS) allows businesses to transfer money from their account to another business, customer or employee's account.

2) The main advantage is that it is an automated method so there is less chance of human error.

3) One disadvantage is that the employee, business or customer needs to have a bank account.

> BACS has replaced cash and cheques as the most common method of paying employees. The employer instructs its bank of the amount to be paid into each employee's bank account. The bank then pays this money on a set day each month or week. The employee is given a payslip which confirms how much has been paid and the deductions made (see page 31).

Payment systems can be a pain in the BACSside...

Examiners are really big on the advantages and disadvantages in this section, so make sure you learn them all — they could earn you a few extra shiny exam marks.

SECTION SIX — MONEY TRANSFERS & E-COMMERCE

Telephone and Internet Banking

Not everyone can get to a bank when it is open, which is why telephone and internet banking have become really popular. Banks like it too because it is cheaper than running bank branches.

Telephone Banking is More Convenient for Customers

1) Telephone banking is used by people who do not have time to visit the bank. Telephone banking lines are open longer hours (sometimes 24 hours).
2) The telephone bank staff work in a large call centre and use a computer to access the customer's bank account details.
3) The customer gives their instructions over the phone and the bank's operator carries them out. Normal banking facilities are available, except withdrawing cash.

Telephone banking is often called telebanking.

Benefits for customers
1) Can access the service anytime anywhere — if they've got a phone.
2) It is quicker and more convenient than visiting a bank branch.

Benefits for banks
1) Call centres are cheaper to run than bank branches.
2) Phone operators can specialise, which makes them more efficient.

Drawbacks for customers
1) Some customers prefer a more personal service.

Drawbacks for banks
1) Employees may lose their jobs in branches.
2) Banks need to have extra security systems to protect against fraud over the phone.

Internet Banking uses the Bank's Website

1) Internet banking can be carried out directly by the account holder, from any computer that has an internet connection. The customer connects to the bank's computer system via the bank's website where they can then directly control their own bank account.
2) The system needs to be kept very secure — to prevent hackers gaining unauthorised access to customer accounts. Customers are required to use usernames and passwords. Firewalls and data encryption are also used (see p.65).

Benefits for customers
1) They can access their bank account whenever they want.
2) It is quicker and more convenient than visiting a bank branch.

Benefits for banks
1) Internet banking is cheaper to run than call centres or bank branches.
2) Fewer staff are needed, so wage costs go down.

Drawbacks for customers and banks
1) Customers need access to the internet.
2) Banks need to prevent hacking.
3) Customers are at risk from phishing.

Phishing is a scam where people pretending to be your bank try to get hold of your sensitive data, like passwords and credit card details, so they can use them fraudulently. It's usually done by email.

Phish and chips — yummy...

Telephone and internet banking have made 24 hour banking possible. Again you need to make sure you know the advantages and disadvantages of this for both the customers and the banks.

Section Six — Money Transfers & E-Commerce

E-Commerce

On this page you'll learn about what e-commerce is and how it is used by businesses. Businesses like Amazon and eBay are e-commerce sites.

E-Commerce is Business That's Done Using the Internet

1) When transactions take place across the internet it is called e-commerce. E-commerce covers a range of activities, e.g. buying goods, selling goods, booking services and online catalogues.

2) Business-to-consumer (B2C) e-commerce is when individual customers like you or me buy stuff on the internet. Business-to-business (B2B) e-commerce is when businesses transact with other businesses over the internet — this is sometimes called e-procurement.

3) E-commerce is very popular in the travel industry — travel agents, airlines and hotels use the internet to advertise their goods and services, to show information about their products, for making bookings and for taking payments.

4) The financial services industry also use e-commerce a lot. Banks offer internet banking (see page 63). Investment and insurance brokers can offer their services, transfer money, and set up and monitor accounts for customers over the internet.

One ticket to Copacabana please.

> Having a website means that a business can provide information about the business and its products. The business can use it to sell their goods or services. It also gives people a way to contact the business.

A Website That Sells Products is Called a Webstore

1) Most webstores allow the customer to either browse through a list of the products or to use a search engine to look for specific products.

2) The customer can select a product to look at more details about it. They can then choose to put the product into a shopping basket — a list of all the products they have chosen to buy.

3) The checkout is where the customer chooses where they want the products delivered and they pay for the products using a credit or debit card.

Setting up a Webstore needs Planning

There are lots of different issues a business needs to think about when they are deciding to set up a website for e-commerce.

1) Firstly a business needs to decide what they are going to sell on the webstore — whether they should sell all their products or just a selection.

2) The webstore needs to be easy to use, secure and reliable. Customers need to be able to trust the webstore.

3) A business needs to decide how they are going to accept online payments. Credit cards are the usual option.

4) A business also needs to have a strategy for marketing the webstore and attracting customers. They can use search engines, banner ads and advertising emails.

Websites, webstores — Spiderman's taking over e-commerce...

E-commerce can help the Sales and Marketing departments to do their jobs. Having a website means a business can advertise its goods or services on the internet and can reach new customers. Also it provides a business with another place to sell, which should increase sales.

SECTION SIX — MONEY TRANSFERS & E-COMMERCE

E-Commerce

To protect consumers, webstores need to be both legal and secure. Different countries have different laws — this page covers laws that apply to websites based in the U.K.

Webstores Need to Operate Within the Law

See page 21 for more on the Data Protection Act.

1) The Data Protection Act (1998) protects the information webstores collect from their customers — data like names, addresses and credit card numbers. It means businesses can only ask for data that is needed to process the order. This data should be kept secure — free from the threat of hackers and fraud.

2) The Data Protection Act says customer data should not be shared with other businesses, unless the customer has agreed. Also the business should not use the data to send unrequested publicity materials — either by post (junk-mail) or by email (spam).

3) Other laws that protect customers are the Sale of Goods Act 1979, the Supply of Goods and Services Act 1982, the Consumer Protection Act 1987 and the Sale and Supply of Goods Act 1994. These laws ensure that goods and services meet three criteria — the product should be fit for its purpose, good enough to sell and match its description.

Firewalls and Data Encryption Help Keep Webstores Secure

1) A firewall is software that makes sure the only data that passes between the internet and the computer is data that the computer has requested and recognised. This helps to reduce the chances of a hacker gaining unauthorised entry to customer data held on the webstore.

2) Data encryption software scrambles the data transmitted between the customer and the website into unreadable code. The webstore computer uses encryption software to reconvert the code back into recognisable data. Any data intercepted by hackers should be unusable.

3) You can tell a webstore is using data encryption if the website address begins with https (s stands for secure). Or if there is a small padlock at the bottom corner of the web-browser window.

E-commerce has Grown Rapidly in Recent Years

Benefits for businesses

1) It can be cheaper than selling goods through high street shops — fewer staff and buildings are needed.
2) It is easier to update the website than to change printed catalogues.
3) It can reach more customers than are able to visit its shops — anyone in the world with an internet connection could be a customer.

Benefits for customers

1) Less hassle than having to visit a real shop.
2) Purchases can be made anytime and anywhere there is an internet connection available.

Disadvantages for businesses and customers

1) The customer needs to have an internet connection.
2) Anyone can set up a webstore — the customer needs to be able to trust the business to deliver what it promises.
3) The website needs to be secure — especially when transmitting customer details such as credit card numbers.
4) Some high street stores complain that customers come to their stores to look at a range of products and then order what they want from a website where it is often cheaper.

7dk![#09 — this gag is encrypted...

Now cover the page and scribble down the advantages and disadvantages of e-commerce.

SECTION SIX — MONEY TRANSFERS & E-COMMERCE

Sales Documents

It's really important for businesses to keep records of the different stages of a transaction. This page is for Edexcel students only. The rest of you can get cracking on the revision summary.

The Supplier Creates Most of the Sales Documents

Businesses like to document all the communications created during a sales transaction. It gives them a record of what has happened and can be referred back to if there is any problem during the sale. Increasingly more documents are being created and stored electronically.

Documentation is usually created for each stage of the sale.

1. **CATALOGUE and PRICE LIST** — A list of products for sale. It is used by customers to decide what to order.
2. **QUOTATION** — A statement by the supplier of what they intend to produce for the customer.
3. **DELIVERY NOTE** — Sent by the supplier to prove the products have been delivered. Where possible the customer signs and returns a copy to the supplier.
4. **INVOICE** — A request for payment from the supplier to the customer. The details should match what was ordered and delivered. The customer usually has 30 days to pay the bill.
5. **CREDIT NOTE** — Issued by the supplier to reflect any differences between what was delivered to the customer and what was included on the invoice.
6. **RECEIPT** — Sent by the supplier to the customer to confirm that the payment has been received.
7. **STATEMENT OF ACCOUNT** — Sent monthly to regular customers. It lists all the invoices that have been sent, how much money has been received from the customer and how much the customer still owes the supplier.

This flow chart shows the order documents are issued during the process of a sale.

- Catalogue and Price List
- Quotation
- Order
- Delivery Note
- Invoice
- Payment
- Remittance Advice
- Credit Note
- Receipt
- Statement of Account

The Customer Has to Produce Some Documents

1. **ORDER** — A request from the customer to the supplier for goods which specifies the quantity, price and delivery requirements.
2. **PAYMENT** — A cheque or other payment method (see Pages 61-62) is sent by the customer to pay the invoice.
3. **REMITTANCE ADVICE** — Sent by the customer with their payment. It helps the supplier to know which invoice has been paid.

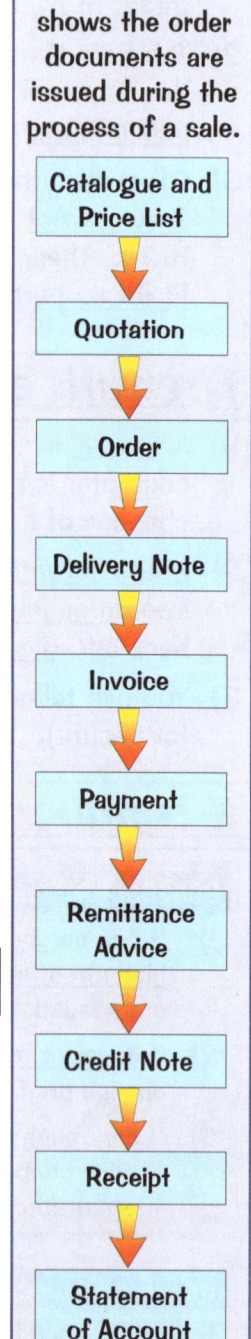

That's not the horse I ordered. Where's that delivery note...

Remittance advice — a very dull advice column...

Yay — no advantages and disadvantages to learn on this page. But there are lots of sales documents you need to know. Cover the page and list all 10 documents and who produces them.

SECTION SIX — MONEY TRANSFERS & E-COMMERCE

Revision Summary for Section Six

That was a nice short section. Have a go at these questions. Once you can answer them all without having to look back at the section, reward yourself with a tea break.

1) Who is the payee?
2) Give one disadvantage of using cash as a payment method.
3) List five pieces of information that are included on a cheque.
4) How long does it take to process a cheque?
5) What is direct debit?
6) What is the main advantage of using direct debit as a payment method?
7) Standing orders are paid for:
   a) a fixed period of time,   b) an indefinite period of time,   c) in cold spaghetti.
8) What is a disadvantage of using standing orders?
9) Give one advantage and one disadvantage of using credit transfers.
10) What does EDI stand for?
11) Give a disadvantage of using EDI.
12) What is the most common method for paying employees?
13) Where do telephone banking staff usually work?
    a) in a call centre   b) in the big brother house   c) in a bank branch
14) List two benefits for customers and two benefits for banks of internet banking.
15) What are the disadvantages of internet banking for a bank?
16) What is e-commerce?
17) Name one industry that uses e-commerce a lot.
18) List four issues a business needs to consider when they are planning an e-commerce website.
19) How does the Data Protection Act protect customer data?
20) What are the other four laws that protect customers using webstores?
21) Explain how a firewall works.
22) Give two ways you can tell a webstore is using data encryption.
23) List four disadvantages of e-commerce.
24) Give three benefits of e-commerce for businesses.
25) List seven documents a supplier creates during a sales transaction.
26) What is a remittance advice?

File Management

It's important that companies have a <u>system</u> for saving work so that employees can find it <u>quickly and easily</u> — time wasted looking for files means that the firm is <u>losing money</u>.

A Good Filing System Makes it Easier to Retrieve Files

Data can be organised by <u>dividing</u> the hard disk into different sections, called <u>folders</u> (or <u>directories</u>). These can then be split into <u>sub-folders</u> (or <u>sub-directories</u>), which contain the individual files. Depending on the type of company, folders, sub-folders and files can be organised by:

1) **OWNERSHIP** — E.g. If a computer or network is used by a number of people, the company may decide to create <u>user areas</u> which only <u>certain employees</u> can use.

2) **CONTENT** — E.g. A building company could have folders for 'Quotes', 'Invoices' and 'Debtors'.

3) **DATE** — E.g. Letters to the same customer may be stored in <u>date order</u>.

4) **SUBJECT** — E.g. A building company may want to keep all the files on new developments by the <u>developments' names</u>.

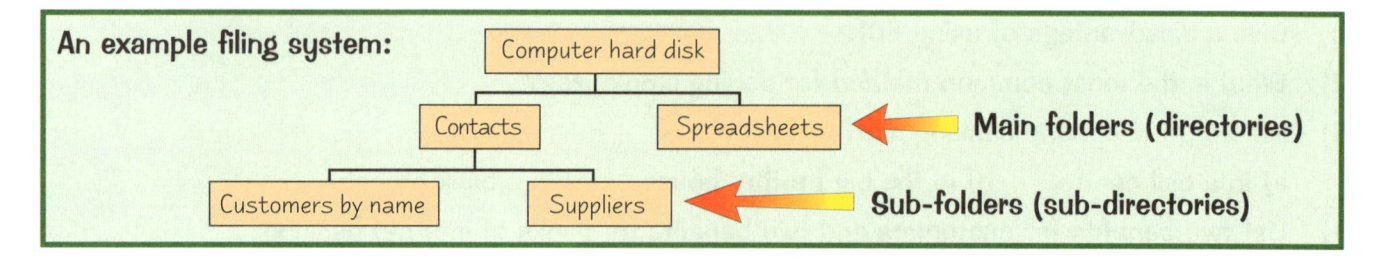

An example filing system:

- Computer hard disk
  - Contacts → Main folders (directories)
    - Customers by name
  - Spreadsheets
    - Suppliers → Sub-folders (sub-directories)

Files Should be Correctly Named and Stored

1) Companies should have <u>set rules</u> about how files are <u>named</u> and where they are <u>kept</u>.

2) When saving files the user must be careful to make sure they are in the <u>right folder</u> and that the file is given a <u>name</u> that describes what it actually is, e.g. 'J Saddique Complaint'. If this isn't done, it will be difficult for <u>someone else</u> to access the file in the <u>future</u>.

The crazy, hedonistic days of the filing cabinet are now sadly numbered.

3) <u>File extensions</u> are the last three letters of the file name, and they show what sort of file it is. They're <u>added automatically</u> when the file's saved and depend on the application the file uses:

APPLICATION	TYPE	EXTENSION
Microsoft® Word	Word Processor	.doc
Microsoft® Excel	Spreadsheet	.xls
Microsoft® Access	Database	.mdb
Microsoft® PowerPoint®	Presentation	.ppt
Pictures	Digital photographs	.jpg

My folders have been stolen — I feel defiled...

It might seem like setting up sub-folders and naming files takes up <u>valuable time</u>. But if you don't do it, you or someone else will lose a lot <u>more time</u> in the future — so it has to be done properly.

Word Processing Basics

You need to know <u>what to use word processing for</u>, its <u>advantages and disadvantages</u> — and <u>how to use it</u>.

Word Processing — it Does More than the Name Says

1) The very first word processors were nothing more than <u>computerised typewriters</u> — they were just used to <u>enter</u> and <u>edit</u> text.

2) Modern word processors are much more powerful <u>computer applications</u>. They combine <u>graphics</u> with different ways of presenting <u>text</u> and <u>numerical</u> information.

> Things a word processor can produce:
> Letters, memos, CVs, questionnaires, reports, leaflets containing graphics, newsletters, printed envelopes, personalised letters using mail merge, worksheets, labels, web pages...
>
> ... and error messages.

Word Processors have Three Benefits

Written documents and documents produced using a typewriter share the same problem — once created they can't easily be <u>altered</u>. Word processors changed all that, and other things too...

1) Once text is entered, it can be <u>processed</u> (i.e. changed) easily. The appearance can be changed — called <u>text formatting</u>. Also the content can be changed — called <u>text editing</u>.

2) The text can be <u>saved</u> and reused. For example, a standard letter <u>template</u> can be created, and used to send similar letters to different people.

3) Professional-looking documents can be created by just about anyone. That's because it's easy to correct spelling mistakes, and to improve the appearance of the document with <u>graphics</u> and text <u>formatting</u>.

I used to be a big shot. Job, wife, typewriter — I had it all...

Always remember your Audience

1) The big <u>problem</u> with word processors is that because they now contain so many different ways to edit and format information, it's all too easy to get <u>carried away</u> and do things just because you <u>can</u>, rather than because it's <u>useful</u>.

> As a result it is **too easy** to GET ✣✧✳✶✩✤✣ AWAY <u>and *let the*</u> technology **get** in **the** way of the <u>mess</u>age. This ᵐᵃᵏᵉˢ things *really* ha**r**d to reᵃd.

Fortunately, here at CGP, we have a highly trained army of chimpanzees working round the clock to make sure nothing like this is ever included in a book.

2) The Golden Rule is to keep the layout <u>simple</u> — remember the needs of your <u>intended audience</u>.

3) If possible design the layout of the document first, and check that the <u>user likes it</u>.

Word processors — even better than quill and parchment...

Where would we be without <u>word processors</u>? They certainly beat a battered up old <u>typewriter</u> which needs a new ink ribbon every ten minutes and has a broken letter 'e'. Praise be to word processors.

SECTION SEVEN — COMPUTER APPLICATIONS IN THE BUSINESS ENVIRONMENT

Text Formatting and Editing

This page covers the basic features of a word processor. You might know how to use them already.

There are Three Main Text Formatting Methods...

1) Change the font (the fancy name for the character style).
   There are two main types of font — serif and sans serif.

   > Serif fonts such as Times New Roman are good for formal letters and reports. (Serifs are the little twiddly bits at the tops and bottoms of the characters.)

   > Sans serif fonts (i.e. fonts without serifs) such as Arial look less formal and more modern.

2) Change the size of the text. Emphasise headings and sub-headings by making them larger. A font size between 10 and 12 point is easy to read for most people (this text is in 12 pt). But small children and people with reading difficulties might need a larger font size.

3) Highlight the text. There are several ways to make text stand out. Words can be in:
   bold type, *italics*, underlined, colour, CLOSED CAPITALS or S P A C E D C A P I T A L S.

   Once again the golden rule is keep things simple — be consistent and don't do them all at once.

...and Four Text Editing Methods...

As well as changing the appearance of text, you can change content as well — individual characters, words, or whole blocks of text. You just need to highlight the bits you want to change.

1) New text can be inserted within existing text.

2) Existing text can be deleted (by using the delete or backspace keys).

3) Text can be moved to another position on the page (e.g. by dragging highlighted text).

4) Text can be copied, so that it appears more than once, or cut, so that it can be moved from one part of the text to another. Highlight the text, select 'copy' or 'cut', put the cursor where you want the text to appear and then select 'paste'.

10,000 lines just isn't the punishment it used to be.

...and Four Ways to Position Text

1) The TAB key on the keyboard makes the cursor jump one step to the right. Use it to start a paragraph away from the side of the page (called indenting). You can also use it to make simple tables — but most word processors have a built-in table facility which works much better.

2) Margins fix how far from the side of the page the text starts and finishes. Changing them is useful if you print pages that are going to be bound together — such as a piece of coursework.

3) Line spacing adjusts how far apart the lines of text are. Double-line spacing is much easier to read than single-line spacing. Bullet points and numbered lists also make text easier to follow.

4) Alignment and justification affects how each line of text is arranged. Three different types are in the box. This paragraph has been justified — so that each full line is the same length.

   > This text is left-aligned.
   >   This text is right-aligned.
   >   This text is centre-aligned.

Non-aligned text is criminal — there's no justification...

Formatting your text appropriately will make your work look smart and professional. But don't go over the top — using loads of different fonts and colours will just make your work look childish.

SECTION SEVEN — COMPUTER APPLICATIONS IN THE BUSINESS ENVIRONMENT

Improving Presentation

Most of the things on this page should also be pretty familiar — but they are all ways of making a document look more professional and readable. Learn all the key terms.

Tables, Borders and Columns can Help Readability

1) Tables are a good way to present lists of numerical or textual information, e.g. lists of names and addresses.

2) Putting borders around tables, pictures or blocks of text helps break up the information on the page — which sometimes makes it easier to read.

3) Columns can be created so that the text flows down the page and jumps automatically to the next column. This is great for newsletters and newspapers.

> **Wordprocessing Weekly News**
>
> Typists around the country were staggered to learn yesterday that text can be arranged automatically in columns.
>
> "I'm staggered," said 38-year-old Ian Denting. "If these newfangled word processors keep going at this rate then I'm going to become marginalised."
>
> Nelson Column, of London, said it had "absolutely nothing to do with me."

Choose the Correct Page Set-Up

Choosing the page set-up means deciding how the page will look when it has been printed. There are two main things to decide.

1) The layout can be either portrait (tall and narrow) or landscape (short and wide).

(With A3, A4, A5 etc., the page becomes half as big as you increase the number by 1.)

2) The size of the paper you want to print on. The page can be A4 (the size of this book), bigger (e.g. A3), or smaller (e.g. A5 or business card size). It's important to have the right size paper — many printers can't print bigger than A4.

Watch Out for Widows and Orphans

Orphans are small blocks of text that don't quite fit onto the bottom of one page, and so get put on a new one. (Widows are the blocks of text they get separated from). As well as looking unprofessional, they waste paper. There are two main ways of getting rid of widows and orphans.

1) Reduce the font size of the entire text so it fits onto a whole page (but not too small to read).

2) Adjust the margins at the top and bottom of the page. However, a page can look cluttered if text is too close to the edge of the page.

A WYSIWYG Screen Display Helps

1) WYSIWYG stands for What You See Is What You Get, meaning that a document will look exactly the same on-screen as on a printed page.

2) Not all word processors are WYSIWYG — others have different ways of viewing the document, and only some of these options might be WYSIWYG.

3) Some views might be non-WYSIWYG to reduce the amount of RAM needed — by not displaying graphics for example.

I never stole those pages — I've been set-up...

It's worth taking the time to find out how to alter all these things on your computer — page set-up, tables, columns etc. Get used to playing around with them until you get the presentation just right.

SECTION SEVEN — COMPUTER APPLICATIONS IN THE BUSINESS ENVIRONMENT

Editing Your Document

To ensure your document is good quality, it should be proofread and edited for mistakes. If you're studying OCR or Edexcel you only need to learn the bottom section of this page. AQA students need to learn the whole page.

There are Standardised Correction Symbols

1) The quality of printed documents affects the impression people have of a business. So it's important that documents are proofread before being printed, to check for mistakes.

2) There's a regular system of symbols that the proofreader can use so that the person making the changes understands what changes should be made.

3) For each correction, one symbol is added in the margin to show the type of correction needed, and another in the actual text, to show where it should be changed.

4) Some of the most common marks are:

MARK IN MARGIN	MARK IN TEXT	MEANING
♂	John isits sat at his desk.	Delete
⋀ when	He fell over⋀it was dark.	Insert
⌒	proo⌒f reading	Remove space
≡	Then i went outside.	Change to capital letter
ⓥ	It was very exciting.	Leave unchanged

On-Screen Symbols can help with Editing Text

1) Sometimes it's unclear how the text has already been edited, e.g. whether a space or a tab has been used. This can be confusing when it comes to editing the text again.

2) Some software has formatting marks which show which keys were used when the document was created. This can make re-editing easier. Some of the symbols used are shown below:

¶ means the enter key has been used to start a new line.

An arrow (→) shows that the tab key has been used to make an indent.

→ We·are·one·of·the·most·successful·pencil·producers·in·the·North-West,·with·numerous·prestigious·clients·throughout·the·region.
¶
¶ → The·company·was·founded·in·1960·by·Sir·Frederick·Flugelhorn,·a·Mancunian·rodent·merchant.

Dots (·) show normal spaces between words.

Typos on the furniture? Time for some pouffe-reading...

Have a go at checking your work with the formatting marks turned on. It might look a bit ugly, but you'll be surprised how much easier it becomes to spot things like double spaces.

SECTION SEVEN — COMPUTER APPLICATIONS IN THE BUSINESS ENVIRONMENT

Word Processing — Advanced Features

These are the slightly fancier word-processing tools — but they're not too hard to learn.

Headers and Footers are Good for Multi-Page Documents

1) These are blocks of information at the top (header) or bottom (footer) of the page. They're especially useful in multi-page documents where similar information needs to be on each page.

2) The most common examples of information in a header or footer include: filename, date and page number. For example, each page can display that it is page X of a document Y pages long — and this is updated automatically if new pages are inserted.

Find and Change Text Using Search and Replace

1) Search enables a specified word to be located wherever it appears in the document.

2) Replace can automatically replace a selected word with a different word — either individually or every time the word occurs.

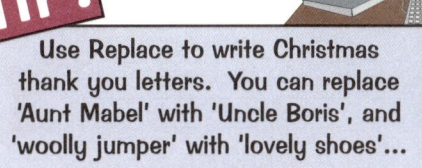

TIP: Use Replace to write Christmas thank you letters. You can replace 'Aunt Mabel' with 'Uncle Boris', and 'woolly jumper' with 'lovely shoes'...

Mind Your Language with Spell- and Grammar-Checking

Most word processors can automatically correct your spelling and grammar.
This should improve the quality of your written communication — but there are problems.

SPELL-CHECKERS:
1) They come in different languages. Many words are spelt differently in different parts of the English speaking world — e.g. labor (American English) and labour (UK English). So if you live in the UK, check that you're using UK English.

2) They only recognise misspelt words — not their context. This is a problem with words like 'were' and 'where'. If you use the wrong one, the spell-checker won't find a problem.

3) Sometimes the dictionaries contain mistakes. One well-known word processor's spell-checker contained a misspelling of 'liaise'.

GRAMMAR-CHECKERS:
Grammar-checkers can be unreliable and give confusing advice. This is because good grammar depends upon context — and most software isn't yet powerful enough to take this into account.

Check Word Count and Readability Scores

1) Sometimes you need to know how many words you've written, e.g. in a piece of coursework. Automatic word counting is an option on most word processors.

2) Readability scores are often linked to grammar checks. The computer counts things like the lengths of words and sentences, and uses them to calculate an overall score. One common index is the Flesch-Kincaid Grade Level score — this gives the reading age of the document as an American high school grade.

Well mice bell chequer is come pleat lee floorless...

These handy little features can all help to make your work more accurate. But don't rely on things like spell-checkers, as they're not perfect — you need to combine them with your own visual checks.

SECTION SEVEN — COMPUTER APPLICATIONS IN THE BUSINESS ENVIRONMENT

Word Processing — Advanced Features

This is the really clever stuff. It could be very useful for your coursework.

You can Write Junk Mail using Mail Merge

Mail merge lets you send personalised letters by combining a standard letter with information in a database. They save clubs and businesses loads of time — and there are three steps involved:

1) A database is created containing the information you want to appear in the personalised letter.
2) A standard letter is created with merge fields, often based on the field names in the database.
3) The standard letter is linked to the database, and software merges the data by inserting each database record in turn into the letter. If there are 1000 names in the database then you'll get 1000 personalised letters — and each one will greet the reader by their surname.

Title	First name	Surname	Type of account	Name of contact
Miss	Laura	Hoar	Luxury	Sam Cox
Mr	Andrew	Corr	Budget	Mark Wanless
Prof	Andrew	Nightingale	Standard	Mikkel Beck

Information in the database

Dear <<Title>> <<Surname>>,
I am writing to inform you of some important changes in the terms of your <<Type of account>> contract. Please read carefully the information enclosed. If you have any queries, please contact <<Name of contact>> on...

Standard letter with merge fields

Dear Mr Corr,
I am writing to inform you of some important changes in the terms of your Budget contract. Please read carefully the information enclosed. If you have any queries, please contact Mark Wanless on...

Letter sent to customer

You can Create Templates of Standard Documents

1) A template is a standard document containing pre-set formats and layouts. Their main benefit is that once they've been created, they save time — so they're often used for business letters.
2) A letter template contains spaces for the recipient's name, address, and the date. These are already formatted — the user just has to stick in the text.

You can Import Information from Other Applications

1) Importing means adding data created using a different software application. A good example is the use of clip-art.
2) In order for imported data to work it must have been saved and exported using a common file format that both pieces of software can recognise.
3) It's sometimes possible to embed a spreadsheet into a word-processed document and then activate it from within the word processor. Or you can link the spreadsheet to the document so that when the spreadsheet is edited, the word-processed document is automatically updated.

You can also link databases and other programs to a word processing document.

This object is embedded in the document. When you double-click on it, you can edit the chart in the spreadsheet application.

Congratulations, Mr <Surname>! You're a Winner!

While reading this page you have been randomly selected to win a large island in <name of sea>, or alternative. To claim your prize just phone 0901 GULL IBLE — calls are charged at £10 a second.

SECTION SEVEN — COMPUTER APPLICATIONS IN THE BUSINESS ENVIRONMENT

Spreadsheets — The Basics

You can do loads of things with spreadsheets. Learn the basics before moving onto the trickier stuff.

Spreadsheets are Clever Calculators

1) A spreadsheet is simply a program that can display and process data in a structured way. Most people think spreadsheets can only process numbers — but they can handle text as well.

2) Spreadsheets can be used to:
    a) record data,
    b) search for particular items of data,
    c) perform calculations based on data,
    d) produce graphs and charts.

3) Examples of uses include keeping records of patients in a doctor's surgery, calculating the exam results of a group of pupils, and producing graphs based on the results of a questionnaire.

Data is Entered into Cells

1) A spreadsheet is made up of rows and columns. These divide the sheet up into individual cells.

2) Each cell can be identified using the column letter and row number as co-ordinates.

The red cell is in Column B and Row 3 — so its cell reference is B3.

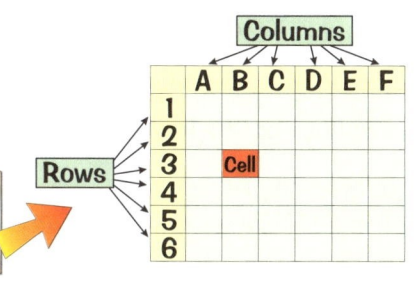

Each Cell can contain One of Three Things

Each cell can contain one (and only one) of three things...

NUMERICAL DATA
e.g. numbers, dates and money. Most spreadsheets recognise dates and money and convert them into a suitable format — so if you enter 23-6, it's converted to 23 June.

TEXT DATA
e.g. people's names, titles of CDs.
1) Column headings usually contain text.
2) One process that can be carried out on text is sorting it into alphabetical order.
3) The ICT term for a piece of text is a text string.

FORMULAS
1) These allow results of calculations to be displayed inside a cell.
2) E.g. you could get the computer to add up all the numbers in a column and display the answer in a cell at the bottom of the column.
3) The great thing about spreadsheets is that if any numbers are changed, the formulas are automatically updated.

The Golden Rule is to put only one piece of data in a cell — this means that you shouldn't mix any of these types of data.

1) If you enter the weight of a kilo of fish as '1000g' then you have numerical data (1000) and text data (g).

2) Spreadsheets treat cells with any text in them as though they contain only text data, which has a numerical value of zero.

3) This means the spreadsheet will read '1000g' as having a numerical value of zero.

The exceptions are things like currencies where the spreadsheet knows that £5 has a value of 5.

Put Data in a cell? What's he done, Warf?

A lot of people find spreadsheets a bit scary. Very few people understand them inside and out, but they're not as hard as they look. Things do get a bit trickier though — turn the page if you dare...

SECTION SEVEN — COMPUTER APPLICATIONS IN THE BUSINESS ENVIRONMENT

Spreadsheets — Creating and Improving

Spreadsheets are used to process data and then communicate the information.

Three Ways to Improve the Design of a Spreadsheet...

1) Put the title of the spreadsheet at the top — normally in cell A1. If the title's too big to fit in A1, it'll spill into cells A2, A3 etc. — this isn't a problem. If a spreadsheet's going to be used as the data file for a mail merge, the first row has to contain field names — so put the title into a header.

2) Next enter the column and row headings. Don't leave any columns or rows empty — they cause problems with charts and graphs. Increase the column width if necessary.

3) Enter data into the cells. Change the cells' format to show numbers to a certain number of decimal places, or with a currency symbol if it's money. Most spreadsheets let you enter data validation formulas — so if you enter someone's age as 1290, you get an error message.

...and Three Ways to Improve its Appearance

1) Format the data in similar ways to a word processor.
   Use italics, bold type, different fonts, colours, sizes etc. to make data stand out.

	A	B	C
	ICT Club — membership fees owing		
2	First Name	Last Name	Amount owing
3	Teresa	Wood	£8.00
4	Tanya	Hide	£5.52
5	Arthur	Brain	£0.00
6	Willie	Winn	£0.00
7	Betty	Wont	£33.67

2) Some spreadsheets allow conditional formatting. The format of a cell is changed if the contents of a cell meet certain conditions, e.g. if a number's negative. Here, the cells turn red if the person owes money.

3) Some spreadsheets let you insert graphics, movies and sounds. This is quite a handy feature — probably.

Data is Easier to Use if it's Been Sorted

1) Sorting data means putting it in a certain order, instead of it just being randomly assorted. Data can be sorted alphabetically, numerically or chronologically (based on time order).

2) It can be sorted by the values in any field of the spreadsheet, in ascending or descending order. For example, this spreadsheet has been sorted by 'Quantity sold', with the highest at the top:

Ref No	Product	Customer	Price per unit	Quantity sold	Total
1.5	Keyboard	Campbell	£12.00	4	£48.00
1.1	Microsoft® Word	Harris	£200.00	2	£400.00
1.4	Microsoft® Excel	Khan	£250.00	2	£500.00
1.2	Microsoft® Project	Hyatt	£150.00	1	£150.00
1.3	Microsoft® PowerPoint®	Patel	£125.00	1	£125.00

3) The table above could also be sorted in other ways, e.g. 'Customer' (alphabetically), or 'Price per unit' (numerically). It just depends on what type of information you want.

Or you can just use lots of pretty colours...

So there are loads of things you can do to improve spreadsheets. You'll never know them all, but the more you know, the better. Spreadsheet data can also be imported or exported — see p.74.

Spreadsheets — Formulas

Without formulas, spreadsheets are just fancy tables. They really put the ace into 'ace spreadsheet'.

A Formula is a Simple Computer Program

1) A formula is an instruction to the computer to process data held in specific cells — using functions which you can either type in or select from a list.

Step 1 — Click on the cell where you want the answer.

Step 2 — Type an equals sign (=).

Step 3 — Type in the formula. Here, it would be C3+D3+E3.

	A	B	C	D	E	F
1	Exam Marks for 1st Year Mocks					
2	First Name	Last Name	Maths	ICT	English	Total
3	Teresa	Wood	63	45	89	=C3+D3+E3
4	Tanya	Hide	32	54	78	
5	Arthur	Brain	33	53	95	
6	Willie	Winn	24	54	75	
7	Betty	Wont	64	53	88	

The equals sign tells the computer to expect a formula.

2) The simplest functions are +, −, * (for multiply) and / (for divide), but there are usually loads of others, e.g. find an average, or the sine of an angle. You can usually choose these from a list.

3) Once you've entered a formula, you can copy it to other cells. So the formula in F3 could be copied to cells F4 to F7 — and the computer would automatically insert the correct formulas for the totals of these rows.

C	D	E	F
Maths	ICT	English	Total
63	45	89	=C3+D3+E3
32	54	78	=C4+D4+E4
33	53	95	=C5+D5+E5
24	54	75	=C6+D6+E6
64	53	88	=C7+D7+E7

The computer changes all the 3s to 4s, 5s, 6s and 7s. when you copy and paste cell F3.

This makes spreadsheets an easy way to do lots of similar calculations on a large set of data.

Formulas can have Absolute or Relative Cell References

1) In the example above, the formula in F3 (=C3+D3+E3) tells the computer to add together the data in the three cells to the left. If you copy this formula to cell F4, it still adds together the contents of the three cells to the left, so F4 becomes '=C4+D4+E4'. That's why they're called relative cell references — the data used is in the same place relative to the answer cell.

2) Sometimes part of a formula will always need to refer to one particular cell — and you don't want the computer to change the cell reference. In this case, you need to use an absolute cell reference — one that won't be changed. The usual way to make a cell reference absolute is to put a dollar sign in front of the cell's coordinates. So B12 is a relative cell reference — but B12 is an absolute cell reference.

3) The spreadsheet below uses an absolute cell reference to represent the % commission a letting agency charges on its properties.

	A	B	C	D
1	Property	Monthly Rent	Letting Agent's	Amount to
2	Oak Vale	£450	£45	£405
3	The Old Post Office	£300	£30	£270
4	Ash House	£250	£25	£225
5	Lilac Cottage	£150	£15	£135
6	Low Wood	£500	£50	£450
7			£165	£1,485
8				
9	Letting Agent's Commission (%):		10	

Column C:
=B2 / 100 * C9
=B3 / 100 * C9
=B4 / 100 * C9
=B5 / 100 * C9
=B6 / 100 * C9

Column D:
=B2 − C2
=B3 − C3
=B4 − C4
=B5 − C5
=B6 − C6

Once you've entered the formula for C2, you can copy and paste it to cells C3 to C6 and it will automatically insert the correct formula.

Formulas — relatively simple or absolutely baffling?

The best way to get your head round all this is to have a go at using some formulas. It'll make a lot more sense, and you'll feel a lot more confident about how it works — it's not as tricky as it looks.

SECTION SEVEN — COMPUTER APPLICATIONS IN THE BUSINESS ENVIRONMENT

Spreadsheets — Graphs and Charts

Graphs and charts are basically different ways of communicating data in visual form.

Creating a Chart is Dead Easy...

All modern spreadsheets can produce graphs and charts — but each one uses a slightly different method. The basic idea is always the same though.

Step One: Get all the data you want to put into a graph into a single block. It's best if the data is arranged in columns.

Step Two: Highlight the data you want to use — you might need to highlight the column headings as well.

Step Three: Select the type of chart you want — be sensible and make sure it's suitable.

Step Four: Choose a meaningful title for the chart — one that summarises the contents of the chart, and label any axes.

Step Five: Decide whether the chart needs a key (also called a legend).

...but you need to know which ones are Appropriate

Spreadsheets can create so many different types of graph — but you need to choose the right kind. Sometimes it's just a matter of taste, but sometimes there are definite rights and wrongs.

1) **Bar Graphs** display a category on the x-axis and a value on the y-axis. Use a bar graph when each category is discrete (i.e. separate from the others) — e.g. the number of people who take certain shoe sizes.

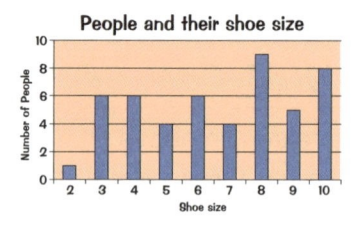

2) **Line Graphs** are similar, but are used when the data on the x-axis isn't in categories — like 'time' when you show the temperature of a room over a 24-hour period.

3) **Scatter Graphs** show the relationship between two sets of data — plot one set along the x-axis and one set on the y-axis, and add a trend line to show the relationship more clearly.

4) **Pie Charts** show the contributions of categories to a total — e.g. a chart showing what I spend my money on.

It's tempting to try to be too clever, and use fancy graphs that aren't really any clearer than something basic. Again the golden rule is keep it simple — make sure the graph gets its point across, and if possible test your graph by showing it to an intended user.

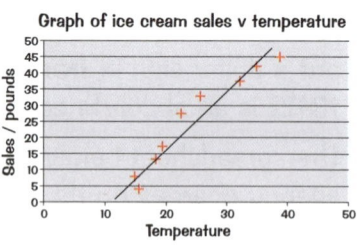

Professor Finkel, several minutes into answering Doctor Smith's question about whether he'd like coffee or tea.

NOOO! No more spreadsheets, I can't take any more...

OK, I'll do you a deal. Learn the stuff on the last few pages, and I'll let you off with only one more page on spreadsheets. Decline my offer, and it's relative cell references for the rest of the book.

SECTION SEVEN — COMPUTER APPLICATIONS IN THE BUSINESS ENVIRONMENT

Spreadsheet Models and Simulations

If you're studying for <u>Edexcel</u> you could get asked about spreadsheet models in the exam.
If you're studying the <u>AQA syllabus or OCR syllabus</u> you don't need to learn this page.

Three Reasons why Spreadsheets make Good Models

1) Spreadsheets use <u>formulas</u> to try to describe the rules of a real-life process. You can put in data and use the formulas to produce <u>output values</u> that suggest what will happen in real life.

2) Spreadsheets can be used to carry out a <u>what-if analysis</u>. This is when the user changes input values to see the <u>effect</u> on the output of the model. So companies can ask a question like, "What would be the effect on profits if I invested this much money in new machinery?"

3) The output can be in the form of <u>graphs</u> and <u>charts</u> to make the predictions easier to understand.

Example 1 — Profitable Pizzas

1) A pizza business could build a <u>spreadsheet model</u> to show its profit from selling pizzas. The owner enters data into cells B1 to B4, then the model <u>calculates</u> the data in cells B5 to B7.

2) The firm could then <u>change</u> any of these variables to see how this would change its profit — e.g. if your production costs went up by 50p per pizza, how would this affect your profits?

3) This could be extended to give a <u>direct link</u> between your costs and the <u>number of pizzas</u> you need to sell to keep your overall profit the same.

	A	B
1	Production cost per pizza	£2.00
2	Other business costs	£1,000
3	Selling price per pizza	£6.00
4	Number of pizzas sold	500
5	Total costs	£2,000
6	Total profit	£1,000
7	Profit per pizza	£2.00

=B2+(B1*B4)
=(B3*B4)-B5
=B6/B4

Example 2 — Queues in a School Canteen

1) A school canteen manager could build a spreadsheet model to represent the relationship between the number of <u>pupils</u> wanting to eat in the canteen, the number of <u>staff</u> and the <u>queuing time</u>.

2) The model could be used to find out the number of staff needed to keep waiting times to a <u>minimum</u>. It could then be used to find out the <u>minimum number</u> of staff needed to serve all meals in less than an <u>hour</u>.

3) The formula in cell B5 is <u>=(B1*B3)/B2</u>.
First it works out the time taken for <u>one person</u> to serve all the pupils (600 × 1 = 600 minutes). Then it divides it by the <u>number of staff</u> (600/4 = 150) to work out how long it will take to serve everyone. It assumes that two people can serve a meal <u>twice as quickly</u> as one person.

	A	B
1	Number of pupils	600
2	Number of staff	4
3	Average time to serve a meal (minutes)	1
4		
5	Total serving time (minutes)	150

4) A <u>weakness</u> of the model is that it assumes that having 4 serving staff means you can serve 4 times quicker. In <u>reality</u>, if only <u>1 pupil</u> can be at the serving hatch at a time, adding more staff <u>won't help</u>. The model also assumes that serving staff can be added forever — but having <u>100 serving staff</u> would create <u>obvious problems</u>.

Wait while I work out if I need anyone to help me.

Mmmmm, pizza...

The stuff on this page really shows <u>why</u> people bother with spreadsheets. They might be fiddly, but in the end you can come up with something that can genuinely <u>help your business</u>.

SECTION SEVEN — COMPUTER APPLICATIONS IN THE BUSINESS ENVIRONMENT

Databases — Creating and Editing One

Yep, it's the page you've been waiting for — <u>databases</u>. Enjoy.

A Database is a Store of Data

1) A database is an <u>organised</u> collection of data.

2) Data is organised into <u>fields</u> and <u>records</u>. The <u>key field</u> contains an item of data that is <u>unique</u> to that record —

In this table, each column is a different field... Key field
...and each row is a record.
Item of data

First Name	Last Name	Department	Payment Number	Date of Birth	Salary	Favourite Fruit
Doug	Witherspoon	Catering	100345	26/09/64	£19,000	Peach
Neil	Beforem	Customer Service	100346	12/08/76	£15,000	Banana
Anita	Dear	Marketing	100347	23/05/83	£18,000	Passion Fruit
Phil	Ordabuk	Sales	100348	30/03/77	£17,000	Strawberries
Bill	O'Verdue	Finance	100349	22/05/79	£15,000	Banana
Stan	D'Alday	Porter	100350	06/11/80	£8,000	Guava

so no records have the same value in the key field — e.g. each employee will have a <u>different payment number</u>, even though they might have the same <u>name</u> or <u>birthday</u> as someone else.

3) The data is entered using a <u>data capture sheet</u>. This is basically a screen where you fill in the details required, which are then transferred into the corresponding fields in the database.

4) The big benefit of databases is that you can <u>search</u> them quickly to find specific data, or use them to generate <u>reports</u> — e.g. which books in a publisher's database have sold the most.

5) You can also update them by <u>adding</u> new records and <u>deleting</u> out-of-date ones.

Well-Structured Fields are Really Important

1) The first step in creating a database is to decide on what <u>fields</u> you need. And once you've decided that, each field needs a <u>name</u>, a <u>description</u> of its contents, a <u>data type</u> and a <u>format</u>.

2) The <u>data type</u> is dead important, as different <u>processes</u> can be performed on different types of data. The most common data types are in the box — most programs allow others.

> **TEXT** e.g. Banana
> **INTEGERS** i.e. whole numbers such as 25
> **REAL NUMBERS** e.g. 25.67
> **DATES** e.g. 26-09-82 or 26/09/82

3) One way to reduce the file size of the database is to use <u>coding</u> — e.g. use 'M' and 'F' for gender instead of 'male' and 'female'. This uses fewer characters and so takes up less <u>memory</u>.

Databases can be Flat-File or Relational

FLAT-FILE DATABASES

1) <u>Flat-file</u> databases are the ones normally used in GCSE ICT coursework.

2) All the data's organised into <u>one table</u>, which can be viewed by opening <u>one data file</u>.

3) Flat-file databases can be created using <u>all</u> database programs and <u>most</u> spreadsheets.

RELATIONAL DATABASES

1) <u>Relational</u> databases store the data in <u>separate</u> tables and files.

2) All the data's linked together by <u>key fields</u> and a database management system (<u>DBMS</u>).

3) The DBMS also controls who can <u>access</u> what — e.g. a firm's customers might be allowed access to information about a firm's products, but not the cost of making them.

4) Relational databases are used a lot in large <u>organisations</u>.

5) A good piece of GCSE <u>coursework</u> might use a simple relational database.

Name	Relationship Duration	Marks out of 10	Best Feature	Worst Feature
Tracy	3 months	4	Personality	Liked Westlife
Penny	1 week	6.5	Nostrils	Her Cilla Black impressions
Charlie	3 days	7	Legs	Moody
Laura	2 years	1	Her sister	Herself
Rebecca	45 seconds	10	Everything	Lack of commitment

Andy's relational database is updated every time he's dumped.

A structured field — cows on one side, sheep on the other...

A <u>flat-file database</u> may well sound like something you'd buy from IKEA, but I promise it's to do with computers. Don't start getting suspicious that this book is just one big furniture-related prank.

SECTION SEVEN — COMPUTER APPLICATIONS IN THE BUSINESS ENVIRONMENT

Databases — Sorts and Queries

As well as knowing how to create a database you need to know how to _interrogate_ one.

Database Records can be Sorted...

1) A _sort_ is the simplest process you can do with a database. You choose a _field_, and the records are then sorted into order using the _entries_ in that field.

2) Sorts can be _alphabetical_, using text fields, _numerical_, using number fields, or _alphanumerical_, combining alphabetical and numerical sorts.

3) Sorts can either be in _ascending_ order (with the lowest value first), or _descending_ order (with the highest value first).

These Fantasy Tiddlywinks League players are sorted in order of transfer value — most valuable first.

First name	Last name	Team	Value
Boris	Batley	Blood and Thunder	£60
Basher	Best	Workington Warriors	£40
Freddy	Beech	Joshy's Giants	£15
Knuckles	Borissov	Higgie's Hairy Men	£5
Smasher	Bentley	Burton's Brigade	£3.50

...Or Searched

1) A _search_ is when the computer looks for data meeting certain _conditions_. To do this, you use a _query_ — which is basically a _list_ of the things you want the computer to look for.

2) _Simple queries_ tell the database to look for records that meet just _one_ condition.

SIMPLE QUERIES
This could be to list all the records of players whose transfer value equals £40 — the query is:
Value = 40.

= finds values _equal_ to a certain amount.
< finds values _less than_ the amount specified.
> finds values _greater than_ the amount specified.
<> finds values _not equal to_ the amount specified.
<= finds values _less than or equal to_ the amount specified.
>= finds values _greater than or equal to_ the amount specified.

3) It's also possible to do _wildcard searches_. These are where you only know _part_ of the value to search for — maybe you can remember that a player's last name begins with 'Be', but can't remember the _full_ name.

WILDCARD SEARCHES
Use * to stand for anything.
In the query
    Last Name = "Be*"
the asterisk can stand for anything (or nothing). So the results will include Best, Bentley and Beech, but not Batley or Boris.

COMPLEX SEARCHES
These search for data meeting more than one condition. You might need to find all the tiddlywinks players called either Boris or Beryl. So your search criteria would be:
    First Name = "Boris" OR "Beryl"
Or maybe you need to find players called Boris who also have a transfer value over £50. In this case the search is:
    First Name = "Boris" AND Value > 50
Or maybe you're looking for people _not_ called Boris whose transfer value is _not_ over £20 (you never know...).
You could use:
    NOT (First Name = "Boris") AND Value <= 20

4) You can also do _complex searches_ — these are when you use _AND_, _OR_ and _NOT_ to find records that meet more than one condition.

5) AND, OR and NOT are _Boolean Logic_ operations. They're used in expressions which can only be either true or false.

Since CD-ROM encyclopaedias and internet search engines work like large databases, most of the ways of searching listed here can be used on them as well.

Get a Cockney database — they're sorted...

Make sure you know the _different types_ of sorts and searches you can do on a database, and when you would use each one. Sadly, wildcard searches aren't as much fun as they sound...

SECTION SEVEN — COMPUTER APPLICATIONS IN THE BUSINESS ENVIRONMENT

Databases — Reports

A report is the <u>result</u> of a database <u>query</u> that is intended to be seen by someone else.

Reports can be in Record- or Column-Format

Reports can either be <u>screen-based</u> or <u>printed</u> depending on what the user needs.

1) <u>Record-format</u> reports display each record of data completely separately. They're useful if you want to view each record on its own.

    This record format report has been designed to be used as a <u>reminder slip</u> to send to customers whose payments are overdue.

    Mortgage Payment Reminder Notice

Name and Postal Address	Account No.
Yoda Murky Swamp District Dagobah System MS5 6RP	07293

Date of Issue:	Amount due
23 June 01	26p

    We have still not received payment of the amount shown above. Please pay this bill immediately.
    If you are having difficulty paying, call us on 1236329012.
    Your hut may be at risk if you do not keep up with payments.
    Offer subject to status. Terms and conditions apply. May the force be with you.

    You can <u>format</u> reports by using different font sizes, colours and so on. If the database format options are limited, you could <u>export</u> the data into a word processor or desktop publishing package where you have more options.

Account No.	First Name	Date of Issue	Amount Due
07293	Yoda	23 June 01	26p
26438	Darth	4 May 01	13p
14472	Luke	23 April 01	68p
91772	Han	5 June 01	84p
02379	Obiwan	23 Dec 01	45p

2) <u>Column-format</u> reports display the data in a big <u>table</u>, with <u>all</u> the information shown underneath the field headings. This is more useful if you're interested in comparing values in particular fields across <u>different</u> records.

    Most database software lets you specify which fields will be displayed in the report.

3) The results of a database query can also be used to create <u>mail-merged letters</u>. E.g. An optician could send reminder letters to all people on their database who have not had an eye test for over 12 months.

    4) Most database software will allow <u>calculations</u> to be performed on the data, and the results displayed as part of a <u>report</u>. For example, a publisher might use a database to store details about the <u>weekly sales</u> of books, with each week's sales in a separate field. The database could then add together the weekly sales for each book and display this on a report as <u>Total Sales</u>.

There are Advantages and Disadvantages to Databases

Advantages of Databases

1) They're a <u>fast</u> and <u>efficient</u> way of storing and accessing large volumes of data.
2) Much less <u>storage space</u> is required, compared to a paper based system, and data is less likely to get <u>lost</u>.
3) <u>Searching</u> for specific data is quicker and easier than using paper records.
4) It's easier to perform <u>calculations</u> and use the database to create other documents.

Disadvantages of Databases

1) Large databases require <u>expensive</u> computer hardware and software.
2) Users need to be <u>trained</u> in how to use them properly.
3) If you store a lot of data you then have to keep it <u>secure</u>.

I'm happy to report that's it for databases...

This isn't as tricky as it looks. Just learn the different <u>types of report</u> you can do, and the <u>pros and cons</u> of databases in general. And I promise there'll be no more Data-out-of-Star-Trek jokes.

SECTION SEVEN — COMPUTER APPLICATIONS IN THE BUSINESS ENVIRONMENT

Graphics — Creating Images

You could draw simple images using a word processor. But for good-looking graphics you need to use graphics software. You need to know the different types of image and how they can be created.

Images are Stored as either Bitmap or Vector Data

There are two types of graphics software. The main differences are to do with how they store the image, and how the image is edited.

A pixel is a coloured dot, and it can take thousands of dots to make up a whole picture.

Painting software (also known as pixel-based software)

1) The graphic is saved as a series of coloured dots (pixels) in a file called a bitmap. These files are large — each dot in a red circle would be saved individually.

2) To edit the image, you basically alter each dot individually, although there are lots of different tools to make this easier.

Drawing software (also called object-based or vector-based software)

1) The image is saved as coordinates and equations (e.g. a red circle might be represented by its radius, the coordinates of its centre and a number for its colour) — making file sizes a lot smaller.

2) The image is edited by manipulating objects (e.g. squares, circles). You can stretch them, twist them, colour them and so on with a series of tools.

You can use Clip-Art...

1) Clip-art is graphics that have been created by someone else, but made available for you to copy. Some come free with software packages — others can be bought on CD-ROM.

2) It's possible to treat the internet as a free clip-art source and copy graphics from web sites. But lots of images are protected by copyright — so using them without permission can be illegal.

...Input Existing Images...

Existing images (e.g. photographs) can be converted and stored as a digital image (i.e. data). There are two main ways to do this:

1) Photographs on film or in a book, or hand-drawings on paper need to be converted into a digital image using a scanner. These images are usually stored as bitmap files — so the files can be very large (though they can be converted to other formats, e.g. JPEGs).

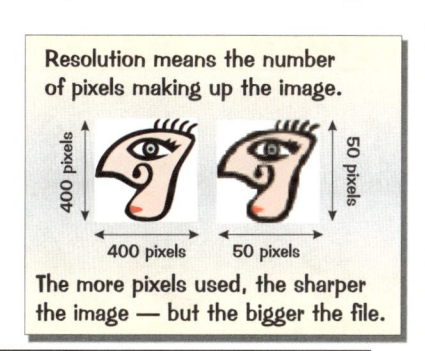

Resolution means the number of pixels making up the image.

400 pixels / 400 pixels — 50 pixels / 50 pixels

The more pixels used, the sharper the image — but the bigger the file.

A JPEG is a compressed bitmap. When you convert a bitmap to a JPEG, you lose some of the picture quality, but it's not noticeable to the human eye — e.g. slight colour changes. Compressing the image in this way can massively reduce the file size.

2) New images can be made using a digital camera, and then downloaded onto a computer. Digital photographs are initially stored as JPEG files — which are usually smaller than bitmaps, although the file size will depend on the level of resolution you've chosen.

...Or Create Your Own

Creating your own graphics by hand using the functions of the software can be very time-consuming — so it's often not worth doing unless there's no other way to get hold of the graphic you want.

One Foot in the Graphics — starring Vector Meldrew...

Now we're getting into the more fun part of this section. There's loads you can do with modern graphics programs, as you'll find out in the next few pages. Let the good times roll.

SECTION SEVEN — COMPUTER APPLICATIONS IN THE BUSINESS ENVIRONMENT

Graphics — Image Manipulation

Graphics software is changing rapidly — especially image manipulation software for digital photos. But whatever the technology, the same basic principles still apply. Learn what they are.

Resize the Object — But try not to Distort it

1) Resizing a graphic is often done after the image has been exported into a word processor or desktop-publishing package.
2) It's usually done by selecting the graphic and then dragging one of the 'handles' — outwards to make the image bigger, and inwards to make it smaller.   
3) The clever bit is to keep the proportions of the image the same — in other words to keep it the same shape. Otherwise the image gets distorted and it can look pretty bad. You'd be amazed at how many publications contain distorted images.

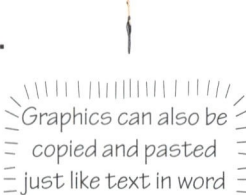

Something's not right...

Graphics can also be copied and pasted just like text in word processors.

Cropping Removes Unwanted Bits

1) Cropping removes parts of the image you don't want — e.g. someone on the edge of the shot you want to get rid of. Cropping reduces the size of the image by removing blocks from the edges of the graphic.
2) It's a quick and easy way to remove bits of the image, although it can only remove whole edges — you can't use it to remove something in the middle of the graphic. Fortunately most graphics software has a separate tool to do this.

I think you cropped my head a bit too much.

Group Two or More Images Together

1) If you want to use an image that isn't in your clip-art library — for example a sheep riding a motorbike — but you have separate clip-art of a sheep and a motorbike, you can make a new object by grouping them together so that it looks like the sheep is riding the bike.
2) You can also select which graphics are at the front of the image and which are at the back — this is called layering.

Rotate and Recolour Objects

1) Images can be rotated to make them appear upside down, or flipped to appear back to front. They can also be rotated by smaller angles, making interesting frog circles possible.
2) Images can also be recoloured — some packages will change the colour of the whole object automatically. With others you have to change it manually, pixel by pixel using a paint spray.

Image cropping — the graphic farmer's best friend...

This stuff is really important for making your graphics look professional. Loads of people who work on all sorts of publications don't know how to manipulate graphics properly — don't be one of them.

SECTION SEVEN — COMPUTER APPLICATIONS IN THE BUSINESS ENVIRONMENT

Desktop Publishing — Basics

Most of the stuff I said about word processing is relevant to desktop publishing (DTP) as well. But you also need to know how DTP is different from word processing.

DTP Creates Professional Looking Pages

1) Desktop publishing software is used to build professional looking pages — ones that are good enough to be published. Rather like this one (ahem).

2) Examples of documents produced using DTP software include newsletters, newspapers, leaflets and posters. But there are loads of others as well.

3) Pages are built up as a series of frames — text frames containing text, graphics frames containing images and so on.

4) DTP software usually lets the user create text and simple pictures — but it often works best when the source material is created in other specialised software (e.g. a word processor or a graphics package) and then imported into the DTP package.

Oh, and Brother John... I need 2,000 church newsletters by tomorrow as well...

DTP Software is usually Frame-Based

1) Frame-based software means that information is put on pages in blocks (called frames).

2) Frames can be moved or resized. This means that it is very easy to edit a DTP document by moving pictures or blocks of text around. Frames can also be moved from page to page.

3) DTP works rather like creating a noticeboard — you have a set of different pieces of information which you can move around until you're happy with the overall layout.

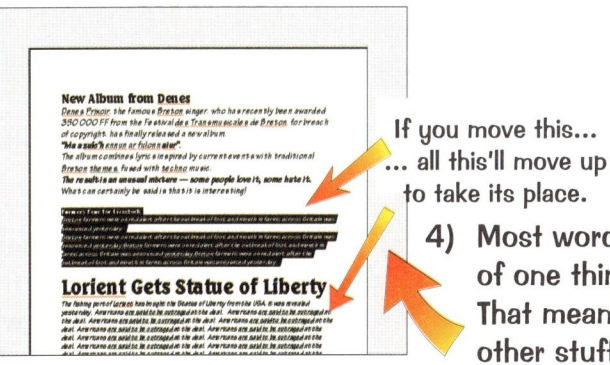

Each block of text or picture forms its own frame that you can drag around separately.

If you move this... ...all this'll move up to take its place.

4) Most word processors are not frame-based, so the position of one thing depends on the position of everything else. That means moving one thing might make a whole load of other stuff move as well. This doesn't happen with DTP.

DTP has Three Main Benefits

1) You can create very professional-looking documents — even with relatively inexpensive DTP packages. But the quality of the printed document is often limited by the quality of the printer.

2) The layout of the document can be changed more easily using DTP than a word processor.

3) The user can control the number of pages more easily than when using a word processor. If there are too many words for a page in a word processor, it will normally create a new page automatically — however the DTP software will usually just not display the text.

Create professional looking pages — like this one...

For a really convincing, professional document, you need to use a DTP package. Word processors will only get you halfway there — they just don't look as slick as DTP. Turn over for more...

SECTION SEVEN — COMPUTER APPLICATIONS IN THE BUSINESS ENVIRONMENT

DTP — Working with Frames

It's the frames that really make DTP software more powerful than a word processor for some tasks. You also need to know how style sheets can improve the layout of a document.

Four Things You can do with a Frame

1) Frames can be lined up in columns — most DTP software can insert column guides or guidelines (lines that appear on screen but not on the printed document) to help position the frames. This keeps the document looking tidy, and the layout consistent.

2) Text frames can be linked together, so any text not fitting inside the first text frame will automatically appear inside the next one. Frames can even be linked across different pages of the document — so they're handy if you want to continue a story on a different page.

3) If a picture frame is positioned on top of a text frame the text will usually wrap around the picture, instead of being covered by it.

4) Frames can be layered — i.e. put on top of each other. This is usually done with picture frames, but can also be done with text frames. E.g. you could put some text over the top of a picture (but you have to make the text frame transparent first so you can still see the picture).

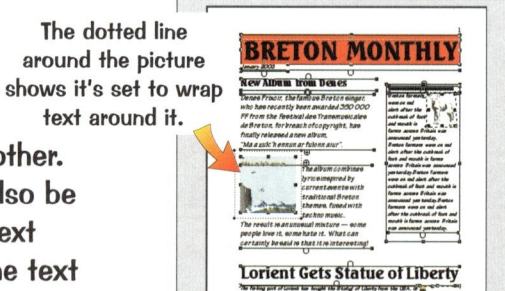

The dotted line around the picture shows it's set to wrap text around it.

Style Sheets and Templates Save Time Designing Pages

1) The Golden Rule of good page design applies to DTP as well as word processing — keep the page layout simple, and appropriate for the needs of the audience. Templates and style sheets can make this easier.

2) Templates and style sheets are similar — they're both files containing the basic layout and format for a standard document. Most DTP software has loads of different templates. They save time but if you're not careful, documents can end up looking unoriginal and dull.

Text box to insert date.

Title already formatted.

Text and picture frames and column guidelines (or guides) already set up.

3) A template for a newspaper will have columns, text frames and picture frames. The text frames will be formatted with different fonts for the newspaper title, headlines and main story.

4) Templates can also be designed by the user — e.g. for a school newsletter. At the top of the template's first page would be the school name, address, crest, and a text box for the date. The basic layout of the other pages may also be set — e.g. a page for PE results might contain graphics to represent the main sports, and tables where results can be entered.

I never killed the DTP software — I was framed...

Templates are another good feature of DTP. If you're making a fairly generic product, you can use a pre-made template. But sometimes it's worth creating your own, if you're after a particular style.

SECTION SEVEN — COMPUTER APPLICATIONS IN THE BUSINESS ENVIRONMENT

Presentation Software

Presentation software is being used more and more to give talks and display ideas. You need to know what it is suitable for and what the main features are. Good news for Edexcel students — you don't need to learn the next few pages, so it's off to the revision summary for you.

Presentations are used to Communicate New Information

1) Presentations are given either to communicate new information, or to help persuade someone of a new idea. A teacher might give a presentation to introduce a new topic in a lesson, or a salesperson could give one to persuade a group of people to buy something.

2) They can sometimes be quite boring — especially if the speaker just talks on and on. Presentation software can help overcome this by using multimedia and animation effects.

Presentations can be given With or Without a Speaker

1) The typical way to give a presentation is with a speaker introducing slides projected onto a large screen. The audience can read the information on the screen while the speaker gives them more detailed spoken information.

2) The other way is to give a presentation without a speaker. For this to work well the slides have to be good enough to communicate all the required information by themselves. Multimedia presentation software can help by allowing a commentary to be recorded.

Presentation Software has Four Main Features

1) Presentation software creates a series of slides in a single document — and each slide contains a number of frames (a bit like DTP software). This means that text and images — and even movies and sounds — can be put on the slide.

2) The really clever thing about presentation software is the speaker can decide when each frame on a page appears — so each bullet point in a list can appear on screen at just the right moment.

3) Animation effects can even make the frames arrive on screen in different ways — e.g. a line of text can appear one word at a time, or the whole line can fly into place from either side.

4) The animation effects can either happen at set times (useful if there's no speaker), or they can be controlled by the speaker as he/she is talking — usually with the click of a mouse or a remote control button.

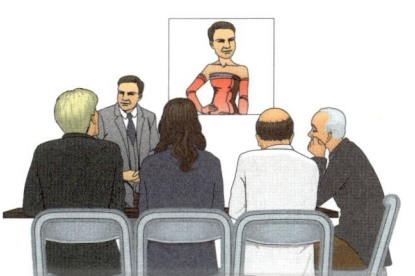

How Presentations Used to be Done

1) Slides used to be either handwritten or word-processed.
2) Unfortunately, it's easy to muddle up the order of the slides.
3) Another problem is that the speaker sometimes has to cover up information they don't want the audience to see yet.
4) Unless the speaker's very good, a presentation can easily end up looking unprofessional.

Wake me up when it's finished...

Presentations have a rather unfortunate reputation for being duller than boiled cabbage. That's why you need to use all the resources available to you to try and keep your audience's attention.

SECTION SEVEN — COMPUTER APPLICATIONS IN THE BUSINESS ENVIRONMENT

Presentation Software

It's one thing to have clever software to produce exciting slides — but it's another thing to know how to use the software to produce a good presentation. Make sure you learn the following rules. (This page is not for Edexcel.)

Remember the Rules for Giving a Good Presentation

1) **PREPARE THOROUGHLY** — make sure you know all about the topic. The point is to get people interested enough that they'll want to ask questions — so you need to have all the answers.

2) **DECIDE ON THE FORMAT** for the presentation — decide whether you'll be delivering it in person, or making it available as a computer file.

3) **WRITE THE SCRIPT** of the presentation first — then decide how the slides will help put the key points of the message across. The slides should be a summary of the main points to be made.

4) **KEEP THE SLIDES SIMPLE** — don't let background colours clash with the text and pictures. Ideally use the same background for all the slides, and don't use hard-to-read fonts. Use no more than two pictures per slide.

5) **USE OPENING AND CLOSING SLIDES** — start the presentation with an attention-grabbing opening slide. The closing slide should leave people with the main message of the presentation.

6) **KEEP EACH SLIDE'S CONTENT TO A MINIMUM** — the Golden Rule is to have no more than six words per line of text and no more than five lines of text on a slide. Font sizes should be big enough for people at the back of the audience to see — between 30 and 60 point should do.

7) **DON'T USE TOO MANY SLIDES** — if you're giving a commentary, each slide should be visible for about two minutes. That means no more than five main slides in a ten-minute presentation.

8) **TEST ANY ANIMATION EFFECTS** using the hardware that will be used in the presentation. Large movie clips might run very slowly on some systems.

9) **REHEARSE** — then rehearse, then rehearse again.

Presentation Software has Pros and Cons

Advantages of using Presentation Software

1) It produces professional looking presentations.
2) Use of multimedia can help grab and keep people's attention.
3) Presentations can be saved and used again — with or without the speaker being present.
4) It's easy to edit presentations and adapt them for different audiences.

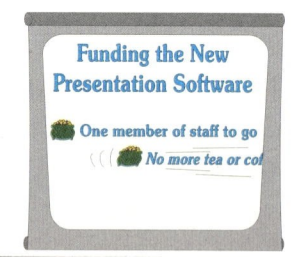

Disadvantages of using Presentation Software

1) It is very easy to get carried away by the technology and produce badly designed slides.
2) The software needs expensive hardware to run the presentation — a laptop computer and an LCD projector can easily cost over £3000.

Funding the New Presentation Software
One member of staff to go
No more tea or cof...

Don't go over the top with the new-fangled wizardry...

As ever, the trick is to strike a balance — use enough to make your presentation interesting, but not so much that people pay more attention to the lovely colours than what you're actually talking about.

SECTION SEVEN — COMPUTER APPLICATIONS IN THE BUSINESS ENVIRONMENT

Project Planning & Diary Management Software

Planning is essential in business. Using ICT helps people in organisations manage their time and communicate plans to other staff in a consistent way. This page is only for OCR.

Diary Software can be Used to Plan Staff Time

Most companies use diary software such as Microsoft® Outlook to keep track of what staff will be doing and where they'll be at particular times. Diary software can be used to:

> 1) Schedule meetings,
> 2) Record appointments,
> 3) Manage bookings of rooms,
> 4) Act as an address book,
> 5) Provide reminders of appointments,
> 6) Some diary software can be used to send and receive emails.

Authorised staff can access the diaries of other staff. This is often used to schedule appointments or visits to customers.

Planning Software is Useful for Making Time Schedules

1) Many companies use project planning software such as Microsoft® Project to help them plan the different stages of projects.

2) From this it is possible to book contractors and materials at the right time, calculate the costs, see where delays occur and replan how to overcome them. They can also show when certain employees' skills will be needed.

3) It is possible to produce a Gannt chart which provides a summary of what should be happening at each point in the schedule. A house builder, for example, may use a Gannt chart like this:

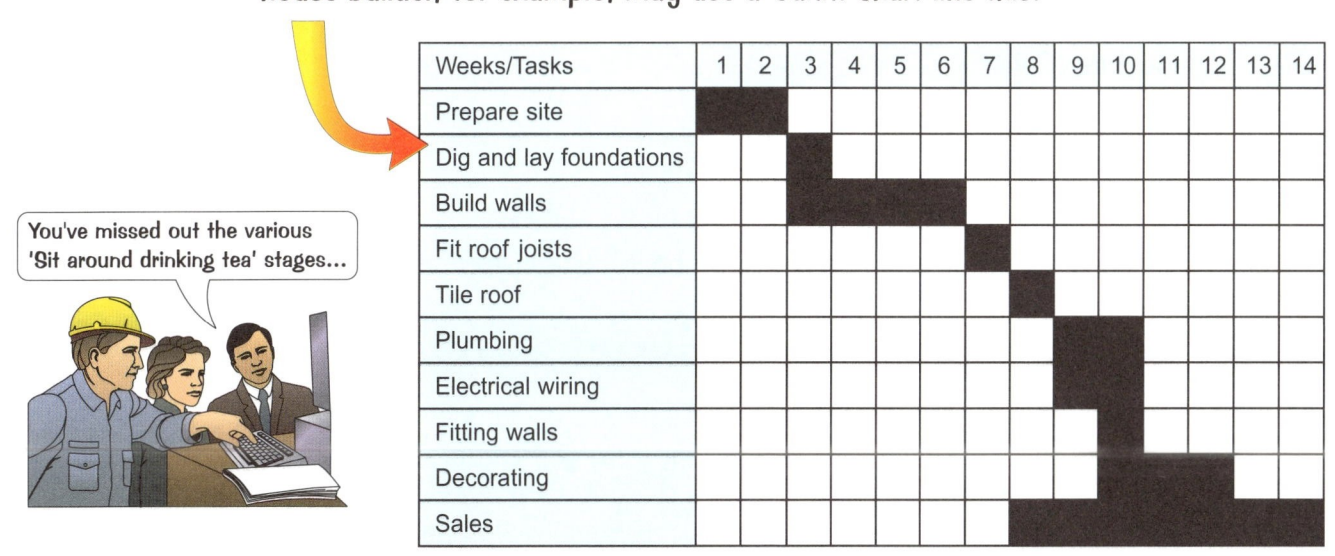

Weeks/Tasks	1	2	3	4	5	6	7	8	9	10	11	12	13	14
Prepare site	■	■												
Dig and lay foundations			■	■										
Build walls					■	■								
Fit roof joists							■							
Tile roof								■						
Plumbing									■	■				
Electrical wiring									■	■				
Fitting walls											■			
Decorating												■		
Sales													■	■

You've missed out the various 'Sit around drinking tea' stages...

Dear Diary, at 10.15 I've got a marketing meeting...

It might seem a bit odd that other people can see what's in your work diary, but there are plenty of good reasons why they can. Just don't go putting entries like 'Job interview at rival company' in it.

SECTION SEVEN — COMPUTER APPLICATIONS IN THE BUSINESS ENVIRONMENT

Revision Summary for Section Seven

OK, that was a long section. Maybe I should have warned you about it, but I didn't want to put you off. And sadly, you haven't finished yet... you must now answer 31 of the most villainous, taxing questions known to humankind, guaranteed to penetrate to the heart of your soul...

1) Name four ways folders and sub-folders can be organised.
2) What's a file extension?
3) List five things that can be produced using a word processor.
4) Explain three benefits of using a word processor to write an essay.
5) Why is it a good idea to keep the layout of a document simple?
6) Give three ways of formatting text.
7) Name four ways of positioning text.
8) What are widows and orphans?
9) a) What does WYSIWYG stand for?
   b) How does it help?
10) What does a ¶ symbol mean?
11) How can headers and footers be useful?
12) Why shouldn't you rely on spell-checkers to pick up all your mistakes?
13) Briefly describe how mail merge works.
14) Describe three types of data that can be contained in the cell of a spreadsheet.
15) What does 'conditional formatting' mean?
16) How do absolute cell references differ from relative cell references?
17) Briefly describe how to create a chart or graph from a spreadsheet.
18) Why might you use a line graph instead of a bar graph?
19) What can scatter graphs be used to show?
20) What is meant by a 'what-if analysis'?
21) What is a key field?
22) Briefly describe the following terms:
    a) flat-file database, b) relational database.
23) Describe three kinds of search you can do on a database.
24) Why might you want a database report to be in column-format?
25) Name three good things about databases.
26) Describe how an image is saved in:
    a) painting software, b) drawing software.
27) Give an advantage of converting a bitmap to a JPEG.
28) What does 'cropping' mean?
29) What benefits are there of DTP programs?
30) Give three ways frames can be useful in DTP.
31) Name three features of presentation software.

Index

A
absolute cell references 77
access rights 19
accident books 12
agendas 38, 45
animation effects 87
anti-virus software 20

B
back-ups 19
Bankers Automated Clearing System (BACS) 14, 31, 62
bankruptcy 1, 2
bar code 14
bar graphs 78
board meetings 4
bonuses 2
brochures 40
bulletin boards 43
bus networks 51
business letters 37

C
call centres 10, 11, 47
cash 2, 61
cash flow 2
cells 75, 77
cellular offices 10
chain of command 35
Chair of the Board 4
charities 1
cheques 61
chip and PIN 14
clip-art 83
column-format reports 82
communication 3, 33-47
communication procedures 47
compact discs (CDs) 55
computer files 18
computer networks 49
conferences 6
confidentiality 21, 46
consultants 9
consultation procedures 28
contracts of employment 26
copyright 20
corporate image 42
credit transfer 62
customer satisfaction 1, 3

D
data capture 13, 14
data encryption software 65
data presentation 17
Data Protection Act (1998) 21
databases 16, 74, 80, 81
debit cards 14
departments 6
desk top publishing (DTP) 16, 85
diary software 89
digital cameras 53
digital versatile discs (DVDs) 55
direct debit 61
disciplinary procedures 26
dismissal 26
Display Screen Equipment Regulations (1992) 12
dot-matrix printers 56
double glazing 11
downloading from the internet 20
drawing software 83
dress codes 28

E
e-commerce 64, 65
editing text 72
electronic data interchange (EDI) 62
electronic filing systems 18
electronic fund transfer at point of sale (EFTPOS) 14
electronic point of sale (EPOS) 14
email 41
employees 1, 3-5, 8, 9, 12, 26-29, 31, 36
employment law 27
environmental factors 59
equipment 12, 22
ergonomics 10
exercise 12
external communication 33, 36, 37, 47

F
fax machines 41
fields 80, 81
file extensions 68
file management 68
finance departments 5
firewall 19, 65
flat-file databases 80
flexi-time 8
floppy disks 54
flowcharts 40
footers 73
formula 77, 79
frame-based software 85
fringe benefits 31

G
grammar-checkers 73
graphics software 83
graphics tablets 52
gross pay 31
grouping images 84

H
hackers 19, 20, 65
hard disks 54
headers 73
Health and Safety at Work Act (1974) 12
Health and Safety Executive (HSE) 12
hierarchy 4, 35
horizontal communication 35
hot desking 9
human resources (HR) 5

I
ICT systems 59
image manipulation 84
importing 74
induction training 29
industrial action 3
ink-jet printers 57
internal communication 33, 36
internet 34, 41, 50, 63, 64
internet banking 63
interviews 13, 25
intranets 50

J
job advertisements 24
job creation 2
job descriptions 24
job security 2, 3
job sharing 8

Index

L
laser printers 56
LCD projectors 58
line graphs 78
Local Area Network (LAN) 49

M
mail merge 74
managers 4
manual filing systems 18
market research 15
market share 2
marketing departments 5
maternity leave 27
meetings 45
memorandum 39
memory sticks 55
messages 33, 34, 46
microfilm 58
microphones 53
mobile phones 41
mouse 52

N
net pay 31
networks 19, 49
network security 19
no smoking policies 28
notices 39

O
objectives 1
off-the-job training 29
OMR device (Optical Mark Recognition) 13
on-the-job training 29
open plan offices 10
organisational structures 5
orphans 71
owners 2, 3

P
page set-up 71
pagers 41
painting software 83
part-time work 8
passwords 19
pay rises 2
PAYE (Pay As You Earn) 31
performance-related pay (PRP) 30
person specifications 24

Personal Computers (PCs) 49
piece-rate wages 30
pie charts 78
presentations 17, 87, 88
presentation software 87, 88
production departments 5
profit 1, 2, 3
project managers 6
project planning software 89
promotion 9
public address systems 43
public limited company (PLC) 4
public messaging systems 43
public relations (PR) 3, 42

Q
qualitative questions 13
quantitive questions 13
questionnaires 13
QWERTY keyboard 52

R
read-only files 19
recruitment agencies 9
redundancy 26
relational databases 80
repetitive strain injury (RSI) 12
reports 40, 82
resignation 26
retirement 26
ring networks 51
rotating images 84

S
safe working environment 12
salary 8, 30
sales documents 66
sales transactions 66
scanners 52
scatter graphs 78
search 73, 81
search and replace 73
selection processes 25
serial numbers 19
shareholders 2
shortlists 25
software 22
sole traders 4
sort 81
sorting data 76

span of control 35
specialists 9
spell-checkers 73
spreadsheets 16, 74, 75, 76, 77, 78, 79
staff appraisals 29
stakeholders 1, 3
standing orders 62
star networks 51
style sheets 86
suppliers 3

T
tally charts 15
taxes 3
teams 6
tele-conferencing 9
telephone banking 63
telephone communication 44
teleworking 9
templates 15, 74, 86
text editing and formatting 70
time rate pay 30
training 9, 11, 31

U
unemployment 2
upper limb disorder (ULD) 12

V
vacancies 24
verbal communication 44
verbal messages 39
vertical communication 35
video-conferencing 44
viruses 20
visual display unit (VDU) 58
voicemail 44

W
wages 30
webcams 53
webstores 64, 65
Wide Area Network (WAN) 50
widows 71
word processing 15, 69
written communication 37, 40
WYSIWYG screen 71

Z
ZIP drives 55